Chinese Religion

THE RELIGIOUS LIFE OF MAN
Frederick J. Streng, Series Editor

Chinese Religion: An Introduction

Second Edition

LAURENCE G. THOMPSON

University of Southern California

DICKENSON PUBLISHING COMPANY, INC.

Encino, California and Belmont, California

ISBN-0-8221-0141-6
Library of Congress Catalog Card Number: 74-83954

This book is dedicated to my Teacher—
CH'EN SHOU-YI

—*Analects,* IX, 10

Table of Contents

Foreword

THE RELIGIOUS LIFE OF MAN series is intended as an introduction to a large, complex field of inquiry—man's religious experience. It seeks to present the depth and richness of religious concepts, forms of worship, spiritual practices, and social institutions found in the major religious traditions throughout the world.

As a specialist in the languages and cultures in which a religion is found, each author is able to illuminate the meanings of a religious perspective and practice as other human beings have experienced it. To communicate this meaning to readers who have had no special training in these cultures and religions, the authors have attempted to provide clear, nontechnical descriptions and interpretations of religious life.

Different interpretive approaches have been used, depending upon the nature of the religious data; some religious expressions, for instance, lend themselves more to developmental, others more to topical studies. But this lack of a single interpretation may itself be instructive, for the experiences and practices regarded as religious in one culture may not be the most important in another.

THE RELIGIOUS LIFE OF MAN is concerned with, on the one hand, the variety of religious expressions found in different traditions and, on the other, the similarities in the structures of religious life. The various forms are interpreted in terms of their cultural context and historical continuity, demonstrating both the diverse expressions and commonalities of religious traditions. Besides the single volumes on different religions, the series offers a core book on the study of religious meaning, which describes different study approaches and examines several modes and structures of religious awareness. In addition, each book presents a list of materials for further reading, including translations of religious texts and detailed examinations of specific topics.

We hope the reader will find these volumes "introductory" in the most significant sense: an introduction to a new perspective for understanding himself and others.

Frederick J. Streng
Series Editor

Preface

I suspect that few authors are ever satisfied with their creations as they appear in print. It is therefore a gratifying occasion when one is given the opportunity to make some improvements. This second edition embodies a number of changes which it is hoped will benefit both style and substance.

The most important of these are first, the inclusion of a new chapter on The Festival Year; and second, expansion of the "Postscript" of the first edition into a full chapter on Disruption of the Tradition. As for the former, it seems remarkable that none of the critics of the first edition should have complained of the omission of this subject; but I, at least, came to feel increasingly uncomfortable that it had received no attention at all. As for the latter, fuller treatment of twentieth century developments is in response to the single most common request of students and colleagues.

Aside from these major additions, the Selected Readings of all chapters have been revised and brought up to date; one change has been made in terminology —the use of lineage instead of clan—to accord with the now commonly accepted usage of anthropologists; and many modifications, larger and smaller, have been made in the text to provide more felicitous expression, to correct questionable statements, or to clarify the discussion. A chart of historical developments, and a selection of illustrations, will hopefully aid comprehension of the text.

Having completed my own revisions, I was then the recipient of a substantial number of specific suggestions from expert reviewers. I am fortunate to be able to improve this edition further through these welcome comments; although to have utilized them all would have necessitated writing a new book (which might have been a better procedure) I have taken those that I felt could be adapted in the new edition. For their kind help I am glad to express here my gratitude to the following: Professors Robert S. Ellwood (and his students), my colleague at the University of Southern California; Willard Johnson of California State University at Long Beach; Spencer Palmer of Brigham Young University; Mokusen Miyuki of California State University at Northridge; Wolfgang Eberhard of the University of California at Berkeley; and Richard C. Bush, Jr., of Oklahoma State University at Stillwater. And of course I owe far more than a pro forma expression of indebtedness to Professor Fred Streng of Southern Methodist University, general editor of THE RELIGIOUS LIFE OF MAN series. His guidance and encouragement have been as indispensable in this revision as in the original work.

With all of this help, despite any shortcomings of the author the second edition will surely be more accurate, readable, comprehensive, and useful to readers.

Laurence G. Thompson
University of Southern California

Preface to the First Edition

According to a notion in Chinese popular religion there is a special section of hell in which teachers who have wronged their pupils by undue leniency must undergo punishment until this heavy sin is expiated.[1] I suppose there must be a similar provision for authors who have the temerity to write very small books on very large subjects. Having committed this sin, I am offering these words as a plea for the defense when the moment of reckoning before the Infernal Judge shall arrive.

Our plea has been hallowed by generations of authors, and is, in brief, that such a book is needed. The subject of religion in China has indeed been treated by many authors, but few, if any, have set out to provide an introduction to the subject in its entirety for the student or general reader having little or no background and no leisure for more extensive study. The literature as a whole is characterized by rather more description than analysis, by limited coverage either of purely literary sources or else of the folkways, and by a prevalence of Western and Christian bias. The more scholarly studies, on the other hand, are at the present stage of research necessarily confined to narrowly defined topics.

The treatment attempted in the present book originates in a concept of social function, and becomes descriptive, analytical, or historical as seems appropriate. I hasten to say that I am far from believing that the results of this procedure represent the ideal. No one could be more conscious than the author of the numerous disputable points that appear here in the disguise of bland assertions. There is also a liberal use of the grand generalization—due in part to limitations of space imposed upon the volumes in the series of which this is one member. These, and other defects which may be apparent particularly to the specialist reader, lie heavy on my heart. But like the translator from classical Chinese, the writer of brief introductions to complicated subjects must often brazen out his difficulties.

The approach adopted, in which the social function of Chinese religion has been emphasized, reflects the author's profound admiration for, and indebtedness to, the epoch-making work of Professor C. K. Yang, *Religion in Chinese Society.*[2] In this book which has for the first time provided us with a real understanding of the nature of Chinese religion, a methodology by the use of which all the pieces of the jigsaw puzzle fall into place.

Two matters concerning which the reader may have questions should be mentioned here. One concerns the historical evolution of Chinese religion. Unfortunately it is not yet possible to deal with this subject satisfactorily. The richness of the documentary materials is inversely proportional to the amount of research thus far undertaken in them. For example, it has been estimated that the Buddhist *Tripitaka* in Chinese is about seven hundred times as voluminous as the *New Testament* in Chinese;[3] yet not even a handful of this material has been translated into Western languages. But that is still more than what we have from the extensive Taoist Canon, which remains virtually unsoiled by the hand of the translator. The history of Chinese Buddhism is known as yet in only the most fragmentary way, through studies which have explored scattered times and topics, while the history of the religious Taoism is hardly more than a hazy outline.

The second matter is the demarcation of religion from philosophy. The very attempt to make such a demarcation is obviously artificial in the case of a culture such as that of China, in which the terms themselves did not exist until contemporary times.* In this book we have expounded the philosophical suppositions underlying Chinese religion in the first chapter, and have stressed what might be called their application in religious forms in the second. Readers who wish further discussion of the more philosophical aspects will be able to supplement this summary treatment with a good quantity and quality of available studies, as indicated in the Selected Readings at the end of Chapter 1.

A book is never the creation of one author alone. I have received much advice and have used much work by other scholars. The end product is far better than my first draft could have led anyone to anticipate. For this help I am deeply grateful. Writings which have been utilized are indicated in the Acknowledgments and the Notes. Colleagues to whom I am indebted for specific criticisms and suggestions include Professors Franklyn Josselyn of Occidental College, Stanley Lusby of Miami University, and Ronald M. Huntington of Chapman College. I am also indebted to the encouragement and advice of Mr. Richard J. Trudgen of Dickenson Publishing Company. It is above all from Professor Frederick J. Streng, friend and former colleague at the University of Southern California, and editor of this series, that I have received continuing wise counsel and firm guidance. It has not been easy to satisfy him—which may serve as the highest praise for an editor.

Laurence G. Thompson

---

*By the time of writing the second edition, I have come to feel that this statement is too extreme. It is in fact possible and desirable to distinguish philosophy and religion in the Chinese tradition, but I mean to say that in the Chinese world view the two were not distinguished as such.

Acknowledgments

The author is indebted to the following for permission to reprint copyrighted material:

George Allen & Unwin Ltd. for permission to reprint from pp. 217 and 269 from Arthur Waley, *The Book of Songs*, 1937.

The Bobbs-Merrill Company, Inc., for permission to reprint from pp. 16, 97, 159, 188, 199 from *The Way of Lao Tzu*, translated by Wing-tsit Chan; copyright ©, 1963, by The Bobbs-Merrill Company, Inc.; reprinted by permission of the Liberal Arts Press Division of The Bobbs-Merrill Company, Inc.

Columbia University Press for permission to reprint from pp. 26, 27, 119 from *Chuang Tzu: Basic Writings*, 1964, translated by Burton Watson.

Thomas Y. Crowell Company and George G. Harrap & Company, Ltd., for permission to reprint from H. Maspero, "The Mythology of Modern China," in J. Hackin *et al., Asiatic Mythology*, p. 340.

Isis for permission to reprint from pp. 67 ff. from Homer H. Dubs, trans., "The Beginnings of Alchemy," Vol. 38, 1937, and from pp. 255 and 260 f. from L. C. Wu and T. L. Davis, trans., "An Ancient Chinese Treatise on Alchemy Entitled Ts'an T'ung Ch'i," Vol. 18, 1932.

B. Karlgren for permission to reprint from pp. 21, 24, 26, 34–35, 36, 39 from *The Book of Documents*, B. Karlgren, trans., *Bulletin of the Museum of Far Eastern Antiquities* (Stockholm), No. 22, 1950.

The London School of Economics and Political Science for permission to reprint from p. 161 from Alan J. A. Elliott, *Chinese Spirit Medium Cults in Singapore*, 1955.

Monumenta Serica for permission to reprint from pp. 9 f., 158 ff., 209 ff. from E. Feifel, trans., "Pao P'u Tzu," Vol. VI, 1941.

Mouton & Co., Publishers, for permission to reprint from pp. 25 f. from Ch'ü T'ung-tsu, *Law and Society in Traditional China*, 1961.

John Murray (Publishers), Ltd., for permission to reprint from pp. 86–89 from Peter Goullart, *The Monastery of Jade Mountain*, 1961, and from p. 43 from Richard Robinson, *Chinese Buddhist Verse*, 1954.

W. W. Norton & Company, Inc., and Walter M. Whitehill for permission to reprint from pp. 9 ff. from Chiang Yee, *A Chinese Childhood*, 1963.

Princeton University Press for permission to reprint from pp. 310 f. and 319 f. from Kenneth Ch'en, *Buddhism in China: A Historical Survey*, 1964, Princeton Paperback, 1972.

Arthur Probsthain, Publisher, for permission to reprint from pp. 244 ff. from Homer Dubs, trans., *The Works of Hsuntze*, 1928, and from pp. 10–11 from John Steele, trans., *I Li*, Vol. II, 1917.

The Smithsonian Institution for permission to reprint from p. 154 from David C. Graham, *Folk Religion in Southwest China*, 1961.

South China Morning Post, Limited, for permission to reprint from pp. 142 f., 144–148 from V. R. Burkhardt, *Chinese Creeds and Customs*, Vol. II, 1953–58.

Mrs. Arthur Waley and the University of London, School of Oriental and African Studies, for permission to reprint from pp. 15 f. from Arthur Waley, "Notes on Chinese Alchemy," *Bulletin of the School of Oriental and African Studies*, Vol. VI, Pt. 1, 1930.

YIN (late SHANG) 'feudal' polity	CHOU feudal polity disintegrates; great states emerge			CH'IN HAN unification under imperial polity

B.C. 1500	1250	1000	750	500	250	A.D. 0

Ancestral cult in royal family ?and nobility. Zoomorphic sacrificial bronze vessels

?Totemism. Elaborate burial sacrifices among elite, including human sacrifices.
Shang Ti (Supreme Ruler in Heaven)
Nature gods.
Astronomical knowledge advanced.
Conceptualization of time in endless sequence ('stems and branches' system)

Great clans develop mythical/legendary genealogies.

Human sacrifice largely abandoned.

Basic cosmological and meta-physical concepts develop: tao, yin-yang, 5 elemental operative qualities (wu-hsing), ch'i (pneuma)

Shu Ching
Shih Ching
Yi Ching (divination sections)

Shang Ti largely replaced by reference to T'ien (Heaven) among philosophers.

Ancestor cult spreads among all classes.

State cult develops in accordance with supposedly ancient practices codified in Li texts.

Confucius establishes moral qualifications of chün-tzu or literatus/gentleman. Tzu Ssu, Mencius and Hsün Tzu shape Confucian doctrines.

?Lao Tzu — Tao Te Ching
Chuang Tzu
(basic texts of Taoism)

Doctrines of Confucian School become State orthodoxy.

but

Age-old magical practices merge with new cult of immortality (the goal to become hsien).

Tales about immortals, living mainly on off-shore islands.

Alchemy (attempt to concoct elixir (wai-tan).

Yogic practices.

Internal gods (body is a microcosm).

'Taoist' pantheon develops. 'Taoist' cults. 'Taoist' communities. 'Taoist' rebellions. Faith-healing most important.

Buddhism enters China.
Texts translated over several centuries, introducing Indian schools. Sangha and Monachism. Magical powers of monks, sutras, images.

TIME LINE OF CHINESE RELIGIOUS HISTORY

Folk religion (the exact nature of folk belief and practice undocumented, but it was certainly spiritistic and magical ● ● ● ● takes on Taoist

SIX DYNASTIES China divided under 'barbarians' (N), and Chinese dynasties (S)	T'ANG re-unification	SUNG	YUAN MING (Mongols)	CH'ING (Manchus)	REPUBLIC (1911—) PEOPLE'S REP. (1949—)
250	500	750	1000	1250	1500	1750	2000

Fêng-shui (geomancy) systematized.

Buddhism enters ancestral cult very early with concepts of purgatory and Western Paradise; soul-masses.

Taoism strongest influence in arts and literature

Confucian influence becomes religiously negligible after fall of Han.

Confucian Canon block-printed (923 - 953).

Manchu rulers stress Confucian ortho-doxy and give great prestige to literati establishment.

Neo-Taoist philosophy ?*Lieh Tzu* (c. 300)

Sung Neo-Confucian philosophy: School of Principle *(Li)* and School of Mind *(Hsin)*.

Buddhist ideas provoke Neo-Confucian response, and strongly color the latter.

Taoist monachism

Chu Hsi's interpretations made State orthodoxy.

Pao-p'u Tzu (317)

Establishment of continuing line of Taoist 'Heavenly Masters' *(T'ien-shih)* named Chang by imperial investment (1016).

Continuing Taoist-Buddhist conflicts

Taoist Canon block-printed (1019).

All Chinese schools completely developed.

T'ien-t'ai
Hua-yen
Ching-t'u
Ch'an
San-lun
(Madhyamika)
Lü

Temporal efflorescence of Buddhism broken by great persecution of 845.

Taoist-Buddhist conflicts; State control exercised with varying degrees of severity over both 'heterodox' religions.

Entire Tripitaka block-printed (972).

From Sung on, only Ching-t'u and Ch'an remained vital schools.

and Buddhist coloration

Ming book, *Canonization of the Gods (Feng Shen Yen-i)* fixes folk pantheon in popular literary form.

Folk religion declines under educational efforts of both Republican governments — except in Taiwan.

Introduction

Chinese Religion and Chinese Culture

The reader, even before opening the book to this page, may have felt some curiosity about the title. Why Chinese "religion" rather than Chinese "religions"? Surely more than one religion has been important in this most ancient of living civilizations? The slightest acquaintance with Asian history will have introduced one to terms like Confucianism, Taoism, Buddhism. However little one may know about these terms, it is at least clear that they refer to distinctive forms of philosophical-religious thought and practice.

It is indeed the purpose of this book to give life to such terms, and in the doing to make apparent the rich variety of religious expression in China. And yet an even more pervasive theme in our exposition is what we may call the *Chineseness* of all these varieties of religious expression. Through the long ages of her history, China has been exposed to many religions, including Judaism, Islam, and the several forms of Christianity, as well as more esoteric types such as Manichaeism and Zoroastrianism. All these remained what they were when they came to China: foreign. The only religion of non-Chinese origin that succeeded in naturalizing itself in China was Buddhism.

Our use of the word religion in the singular is intended, then, to convey our interpretation that the character of religious expression in China is above all *a manifestation of the Chinese culture.* To attempt to understand religion in China as several systems of doctrine is to read Western experience into a quite different set of circumstances. Creed—what one *believes*—is the crux of the matter in the West; the religion of China knows no credo. In the past almost every member of Western society belonged to some religious sect, each sect being distinguished from others by its insistence upon certain doctrinal propositions. In China lay people did not belong to an institutionalized sect, nor did their religious life have anything to do with signing articles of faith. Except in the case of the professional religious living apart in monasteries, religion in China was so woven into the broad fabric of family and social life that there was not even a special word for it until modern times, when one was coined to match the Western term.

Most significantly of all, in the West the development of religion was closely bound up with the lively history of ideas. Because of the central place of doctrine in religion, it necessarily shared in the questionings, the changing insights, the disputations, and the actual warfare of the Western world of ideas. Philosophers, theologians, and scientists endlessly pondered and argued and revised the hypotheses upon which sectarian tenets were based. But in China, not only did doctrinally founded churches not exist, but the world view and the ethic did not undergo such restless revisions. Even the impact of Buddhism, which began at about the time of the Christian era, failed to change materially the fundamental Chinese outlook. Instead, after a thousand years, Buddhism itself was largely accommodated to these ingrained views.

Because of these facts, we have thought that the most meaningful introduction to Chinese religion is one which stresses, first, the world view that finds expression in religion and, second, the functioning of religious expression in Chinese society. The world view and the society here pictured are those generally characteristic of China during the past two thousand years. In a final chapter we have given a brief description of the changes being wrought in this great tradition by the circumstances of the most recent century. Such changes are certainly far reaching, but we are as yet too close to the processes to be able to predict the outcome. In any case, the developments of the contemporary period can only be understood in their relationship to the traditional religion; and that traditional religion, far from having passed from the scene, is still very lively.

SELECTED READINGS

The items listed as selected readings are necessarily very limited. They include materials
    that are considered most useful to the purposes of this book, and almost all of them
    are in English. Readers desiring to pursue various aspects of the subject in greater
    depth should consult the following work:

Laurence G. Thompson, *Studies of Chinese Religion: A Comprehensive and Classified
    Bibliography of Publications in English, French, and German through 1970.* San
    Antonio, Tex.: Trinity University Press, 1975.

Historical treatments of Chinese religion have been attempted in:

Hughes, E. R., and K. Hughes, *Religion in China.* London: Hutchinson's University
    Library, 1950. Brief, authoritative survey.

Smith, D. Howard, *Chinese Religions.* New York: Holt, Rinehart, and Winston, 1968. The
    first six chapters are much more satisfactory than the remainder.

The basic work that should be utilized in any serious study is:

Yang, C. K., *Religion in Chinese Society.* Berkeley and Los Angeles: University of Califor-
    nia Press, 1961; papercover available.

An anthology of readings especially compiled as a companion to the present book is:

Laurence G. Thompson, *The Chinese Way in Religion.* Encino, Calif. and Belmont, Calif.:
    Dickenson Publishing Co., Inc., 1973.

1.
The World View of Chinese Philosophy

Nature

The Naturalistic Universe. The universe of the ancient Chinese was naturalistic, in the sense that it was characterized by the regularity that Western philosophy has called "law"—*but it lacked the Western assumption of an outside "lawgiver."*[1] Three features of this regularity were conspicuous to the ancients: first, the cyclical processes, such as night following day followed by night, or the rotation of the seasons; second, the process of growth and decline, exemplified by the waxing and waning of the moon; third, the bipolarity of nature. The latter meant not simply that everything had its opposite, but that opposites were necessary and complementary to each other. These opposites tended to merge into each other, and even to become each the opposite of its former self. The ground or fundamental stuff of the universe was seen to be homogeneous, and all particular phenomena were individualized through these processes. The bipolarity of nature was no doubt the latest to be grasped as a principle, being by far the most sophisticated.

In fact, once this third principle was recognized it could be seen to account for the other two, which were merely its operational aspects. As a principle, it was one of the most fruitful and useful ever devised by the mind of man for making sense out of the infinite multitude of diverse facts in the universe. Today, described as positive and negative electrical charges, it is the basis of "matter" according to science (we are not suggesting that the ancient Chinese knew about electricity); in traditional China, expressed through the concepts of *yin* and *yang,* bipolarity constituted the specific characteristic of Chinese metaphysics. Once this principle had suggested itself, perhaps as early as 1000–500 B.C., the Chinese were able to develop a perfectly coherent theory of the cosmos. Nature was seen to operate through the interplay of light and darkness, heat and cold, male and female, and so forth. The *yang* (as represented by the first of each pair) and *yin* (the second of each pair) were not in absolute and permanent opposition to each other. They might best be described as definable phases in a ceaseless flow of change:

> When the sun goes the moon comes; when the moon goes the sun comes. The sun and moon give way to each other and their brightness is produced. When the cold goes the heat comes; when the heat goes the cold comes. The cold and heat give way to each other and the round of the year is completed. That which goes wanes, and

that which comes waxes. The waning and waxing affect each other and benefits are produced.[2]

It is significant that this bipolar world view did not, in its ancient, classical formulation, have anything to do with a struggle between basic principles of good and evil. *Yin and yang* were equally essential forces in the ceaseless dynamic of an impersonal universe.

In the material world produced through this process there was an infinite variety of phenomena, and the Chinese by late Chou times (fifth-third centuries B.C.)* had, like other ancient peoples, overcome this confusion by classifying all things into what seemed to be irreducible elements. As a consequence of the principle of constant transformation embodied in the *yin-yang* theory, the Chinese concept of the primary elements focused on the fundamental *qualities* observed in things. These qualities were not static, but were ceaselessly interacting, transforming, and replacing each other. The Chinese word *hsing,* which has customarily been translated as "element," is actually a verb meaning to walk, to go, to act. There were five *hsing,* given in the "Hung Fan" chapter of *Shu Ching*[3] (see appendix) as water, fire, wood, metal, and earth (their order and mutual reactions differ in other texts). Thinking of *hsing* as verbal will help us to keep in mind their active nature (water overcoming fire, fire burning wood, and so forth); while thinking of *hsing* as adjectival will help us to understand their elemental nature (that is, all things may be categorized as either "watery," i.e., liquid; "fiery," i.e., gaseous; and so forth). So as to emphasize both of these aspects of the Chinese term, we shall throughout this book refer to the *hsing* as the *five operational qualities.*

The Supreme Ruler in Heaven. Although the universe thus functions through the workings of "law without a lawgiver," there is at the same time a personalized power of conspicuous importance in the thinking of the ancient Chinese. At the dawn of their history, twelve centuries before the Christian era, the writing on oracle bones (p. 34) and ritual bronze vessels, as well as the somewhat later texts preserved in *Shu Ching* and *Shih Ching* (see appendix), speak frequently of a Supreme Ruler in Heaven called *ti, shang ti,* or *t'ien. Ti* is written with a graph that later becomes a title of the Chinese emperor, while *shang ti* means the superior *ti,* or the *Ti*-on-High. These appellations have often been rendered by translators as "God." *T'ien* is a word that has the simple meaning of sky, and the more pregnant meaning of heaven. In its latter significance it is happily rendered in English with the capital letter, for of course we commonly substitute Heaven for God in such expressions as "Heaven help me!" or "Heaven only knows!" It is *t'ien* which eventually becomes the customary term for the Supreme Ruler, and this shows very well the impersonal character the latter gradually came (by the last two or three centuries of the Chou dynasty) to assume in the

*For dates of the dynasties into which Chinese history is conventionally divided see Table of Chinese Religious History preceeding the Introduction.

Chinese mind. *Ti* lost its connotation of the Highest, and became an appellation not only of the earthly emperor, but of deities subordinate to Heaven.

Nevertheless *shang ti* was retained as the name, or part of the name, of the Supreme Ruler in Heaven in the worship performed by the emperor in postfeudal (that is, after Chou) times. The question as to the correct connotation of these Chinese terms remains open despite several centuries of discussions and investigations by Western scholars. Our view is that the Supreme Ruler in Heaven, while the highest deity, is not equivalent to the God of Western religion or philosophy. Like the Old Testament Jehovah, *shang ti* or *t'ien* is pictured in the ancient texts as being concerned with the actions of man, and as the source of the "mandate" from which the ruling dynasty receives its legitimacy. From *shang ti* or *t'ien* come blessings and punishments. But there is no hint that he is the Creator of the universe or the Cause of its functioning. Like Jehovah the Chinese Supreme Ruler is a tribal god, and indeed one plausible interpretation is that the term *ti* or *shang ti* actually means the High Ancestor of the ruling house. It is only later, when the depersonalized *t'ien* becomes the Highest in a trinity of Heaven, Earth, and Man, that we might ascribe a God-like power to the Supreme Ruler. And yet even this Heaven of later times is not the Ultimate or the Absolute. For that we must look into another term, the famous *tao*.

Tao. This is such an important word in Chinese thought that translators have often felt it best to leave it in transliterated form. Key terms in any great tradition are inevitably distorted or even falsified by translation, and can be grasped in something like their true significance only by seeing their operation in many contexts. In studying Buddhism, for example, such words as *nirvāṇa* and *śūnyatā* are rightly considered as technical terms and customarily left untranslated. This may well be the best way to treat *tao*.

For our purposes it will be sufficient to explain that there are two general applications of this term in Chinese thought. The first is fortunately easy to appreciate because it is a metaphor which we also use: from the commonplace meaning of a road, path, or way, the analogy is drawn of a Way, or *the* Way. In this usage *tao* refers to truth—ethical, religious, or other—and in terms of conduct it means the normative standard:

> The Master said, "*Tao* is not far from man. If what one takes to be *tao* is far from man, it cannot be considered [the true] *tao*."[4]

This passage from *Chung Yung* (see appendix) is rendered into English by Ku Hung-ming,* a scholar with an excellent command of English, in such a way as to bring out fully this sense of *tao:*

> Confucius remarked: "The actual moral law is not something away from the actuality of human life. When men take up something away from the actuality of human life as the moral law, that is not the moral law."[5]

*Note that Chinese always give surname first; the given name follows, either a single word, or a double name hyphenated.

One other example, from *Analects* (see appendix), will suffice:

The Master said, "Shen, my *tao* is unified by a single [principle]. . . . When the Master
went out, the [other] disciples asked, "What did he mean?" Tseng Tzu replied, "The
tao of our Master is only *chung* and *shu*."⁶ (Shen was the personal name of the
disciple Tseng Tzu. *Chung* is usually translated as loyalty or conscientiousness and
shu as reciprocity.)

The second sense of *tao* is more specifically pertinent to understanding the
Chinese world view. It is this sense that has been made most famous by the
often-translated text called *Tao Te Ching,* traditionally attributed to a somewhat
older contemporary of Confucius named Lao Tzu (sixth century B.C.). But although *tao* was such a central concept to Lao Tzu and his school that it gave its
name to that school, it is by no means the exclusive property of the Taoists. *Tao*
in the sense we are discussing is from one point of view that regularity of operation
in the universe which has earlier been noted. But it is more: it is the reality behind
or within appearances, the ultimate metaphysical truth. Like the God of some
Western philosophers or the Void (*śūnyatā*) of Mahāyāna Buddhism, it is that
about which nothing can be predicated, but because of which all particular
phenomena have their being. The opening lines of *Tao Te Ching* struggle to put
this essentially inexpressible concept into words:

The Tao that can be told of is not the eternal Tao;
The name that can be named is not the eternal name.
The Nameless is the origin of Heaven and Earth;
The Named is the mother of all beings.

Therefore let there always be non-being, so we may see their subtlety,
And let there always be being, so we may see their outcome.
The two are the same,
But after they are produced, they have different names.
They both may be called deep and profound,
Deeper and more profound,
The door of all subtleties!⁷

Without going any further into various metaphysical interpretations of *tao,*
we summarize by saying that *tao* might be likened to the Laws of Nature, or
better to Nature itself. And whether taken as Being or as Nonbeing, or as the
Principle in all particular things, it is in any case never conceived as Deity.

Supernatural Beings. There is thus perhaps no real Deity with the capital letter
to be equated with the God of Western religion. We have seen that Heaven
eventually becomes the term customarily used for the Supreme Ruler, but we now
know that behind or beyond heaven there are the workings of *yin* and *yang* which
have their source in *tao.* Such would be the metaphysical view of sophisticated
minds. It is probable that a few of these minds were in all ages able to content
themselves with such an abstract theory, but certainly most, even of these educated elite, shared to some extent the belief in supernatural powers prevailing

among the great masses of the people. Not *tao,* and not the one, omnipotent God of Western monotheism, but a countless host of greater and lesser deities accounted in the popular mind for what went on in this world.

There is nothing distinctively Chinese in the way whereby the forces of nature were personified or the heavenly bodies were believed to exercise a direct influence in human affairs, or the way in which otherwise inexplicable occurrences of disease and other misfortunes were attributed to malignant spirits. The deification of human beings characteristic of both family and folk religion is somewhat more exceptional, although not unique. These matters will be taken up in later chapters. Here we wish only to underline the point that in the Chinese world view there was *an unseen but completely real dimension to the world: that of the spiritual beings.* This was the dimension in which the deified ancestors dwelt, and it was the dimension inhabited by the malevolent ghosts of those whose sacrifices had been discontinued, or who had otherwise been wronged in their earthly term. The malevolent ghosts sought revenge on mortals, and much of the popular religion was concerned with protection against their attacks. Charms, exorcism, communication through mediums, sounding of gongs and firecrackers, placing of spirit-walls to prevent entry of evil spirits through a doorway, offerings to placate them, the burning of incense, prayers, fasting—the long catalogue of such practices gives ample evidence of the reality of dangers to man from the spiritual dimension.

A Gestalt Cosmology. The total world view of the popular religion may thus not unreasonably be called animistic. While the spirits were most importantly those of human beings, there was no lack of other spirits such as those of animals, plants, and nonorganic objects including stones and stars, rivers and mountains. And although the educated intelligentsia would certainly not hold the more naïve and crude notions of the peasant populace, they did share the same general outlook, at least to the extent that they never set man and nature apart.

To modern man in the West it must require a great effort of the imagination to empathize with the traditional Chinese feeling. We are so accustomed to seeing the physical world as something "out there," as an environment (mostly hostile to us), or as a purely material object for our exploitation, that we can scarcely comprehend the Chinese sense of the wholeness of the universe, in which man is a part, only a part, and really a part. This intimate feeling of being at home in nature is shown in many ways in the traditional Chinese culture: in the philosophical writings, particularly the wonderful flights of Chuang Tzu (365–290 B.C.), as a perennial theme of poetry through the ages, and visually in those landscape paintings which place man in perspective as a tiny observer of the vast universe—an observer who is seeking to absorb himself therein.

In an integrated universe, it will occur to men to seek out the signs writ large in nature whereby they may confirm that human actions are in accord or discordant with the *tao* of this universe. In the *Shu Ching* we may read how these signs were interpreted by the Chou people:

... the various verifications ... are called rain, sunshine, heat, cold, wind and their seasonableness; when the five come in a complete way, and each in its order, all the plants are rich and luxuriant. If one (of them) is complete to the extreme, it is baleful; if one is lacking to the extreme, it is baleful. (Some) are called the lucky verifications. Gravity—seasonable rain responds to it; orderliness—seasonable sunshine responds to it; wisdom—seasonable heat responds to it ... (Some) are called unlucky verifications. Wildness—constant rain responds to it; incorrectness—constant sunshine responds to it; indolence—constant heat responds to it. ...

... What the king scrutinizes is the year (sc. as to its natural phenomena), the dignitaries and noblemen the months, the many lower officials the days (sc. for verification of their government). When in years, months and days the seasonableness has no ... failing, the ... many cereals ripen, the administration is enlightened, talented men of the people are distinguished, the house is peaceful and at ease. ... What the common people scrutinize is the stars. There are stars which favour wind, there are stars which favour rain. ... According as the moons follow the (various) stars, there is wind and rain (sc. the people can judge the indications in the sky and so participate in the "verifications").[8]

The same text in another section gives a clear illustration of the specific application of the theory:

In the autumn, when there was great ripeness, when they had not yet reaped, Heaven made great thunder and rain with wind, all the grain laid itself down, great trees were uprooted. The people of the land greatly feared ... (The cause was discovered to be a calumniation of the king's uncle, Regent Chou Kung. Thereupon the king said, weeping:) Formerly the prince (i.e., Chou Kung) toiled for the Royal house, but I, young man, have not ... had the means of knowing it. Now Heaven has set in motion its terror in order to signalize Chou Kung's virtue. I, the little child, will in person go and meet him ... When the king came out to the suburbs (sc. on his way to meet Chou Kung), Heaven rained and turned the wind and the grain all rose up. The two princes ordered the people of the state, in regard to all great trees which had been overthrown, to raise them all and earth them up. The year was then greatly ... fruitful.[9]

Such a belief in the interactions of man (particularly represented in the person of the Son of Heaven, as the king was titled) and the rest of nature continued to be a basic aspect of the Chinese world view up to modern times. The reading of omens and portents was a pronounced feature of the Chinese religion.

It is surely this "gestalt cosmology" that gives to the world view of the native Chinese tradition its specific character. Lacking the premise of a God "out there" who created and controls the universe and requires man's worship, the typical Western form of religion did not develop. Lacking the theory that human souls are particularizations of the universal Brahman, the typical Indian form of religon likewise did not develop. The Chinese religion, based on the premises we have outlined, developed on its highest level a mysticism perhaps not essentially different from the mysticisms of other religions, but nevertheless felt to be identification with *tao*, or Nature itself, and not with God, beyond or outside of Nature. The

Chinese religion, while giving to Heaven power to punish man's misbehavior, defined this misbehavior as actions inimical to the harmonious workings of the universe. The Chinese religion conspicuously lacked the central concept of the ever-brooding presence of Almighty God, continuously attending to the sins and virtues of every individual, swift to save or damn, requiring submission, belief, faith, and adoration.

Man

Theory of the Soul. In view of the central place of ancestor worship in Chinese culture (which we shall examine in detail later on) one might suppose that a systematic rationale would have been developed to clarify the nature of the soul. The Western mind has always felt the necessity for logical "proofs" of such things, and the Western religion emphasizes doctrine. The Chinese mind, however, did not feel this compulsion to formulate speculative systems, and Chinese ideas concerning the soul must be gleaned from here and there, never having received any thoroughgoing formal treatment.

Although we have no way of knowing the age in which the Chinese began to formulate their specific notions concerning the human soul, it is obvious from the fact that ancestor worship was already a fully developed cult at the dawn of history that survival beyond death was the accepted belief. For literary evidences concerning this belief we have to rely upon the same books we have already cited, as well as others that made their appearance in late Chou times. From these sources we discover that the ideas about the soul and its survival emerge from the general cosmological views already outlined above.

In this way of thinking the human being, like every other thing in the universe, is a product of the operations of *yin* and *yang*—most obviously in fact, since new life is produced through the union of the male and female. This reduces the status of human souls to something less exalted than that assumed in India or the West. Men are not the special creations of God, much less are they God Himself. In the Taoist philosophers, most picturesquely in Chuang Tzu (365–290 B.C.), the Chinese naturalism is expressed in its most extreme form:

> Tzu Lai fell ill, and laid [*sic*] gasping at the point of death, while his wife and children wept around him. Tzu Li went to see him, and said to the wife and children: "Go, hush, get out of the way. Do not disturb the natural evolution." Then, leaning against the door, he said: "Great is nature! What will she make of you? Will she make you into the liver of a rat? Will she make you into the arm of an insect?"

> "Wherever a parent tells a son to go," replied Tzu Lai, "east, west, south, or north, he simply follows the command. Nature, the Yin and Yang, is no other than a man's parent. If she bid me die quickly, and I demur, then I am obstinate and rebellious; she does no wrong. The universe carries me in my body, toils me through my life, gives me repose with old age, and rests me in death. What makes my life a good makes my death a good also. Here is a great foundryman, casting his metal. If the metal should leap up and say: 'I must be made into a sword, I must be made into a sword,'

the great foundryman would certainly regard it as uncanny. Now if I, who once meet the human form, were to say: 'I must be a man, I must be a man,' the Maker of things would certainly regard me as uncanny. If we take the universe as a great melting pot, and nature as a great foundryman, what place is it not right for us to go? Calmly we die; quietly we live."[10]

In this view it may be said that there is really no room at all for the soul. *Tao*, functioning through the operations of *yin* and *yang*, produces both grosser, material manifestations, and subtler, spiritual manifestations. Man is a combination of these, and upon his death the former would return to Earth (which is *yin*) while the latter would ascend to the bright, ethereal region of Heaven (which is *yang*). Although there seems to be a dualism in the human constitution, it thus differs from the dualism of body and soul that has plagued the Western philosophers. Perhaps the human constitution in this Chinese concept could be likened to a mixture in a test tube. During life it is by vigorous activity kept in stable solution, but with the cessation of that activity due to death it separates out, the coarser components settling to the bottom, leaving the pure liquid above.

But all this is too abstract to satisfy the common need for a more comforting theory, a theory certainly required for ancester worship. In China as elsewhere, the vulgar notion of the soul would be that of a pale shadow of the living man, usually invisible, but capable of horrifying people occasionally in appearing before them as a grotesque caricature of his mortal form. Such ghostly apparitions have been a staple of Chinese stories from early Chou times to the present. However, there was a distinction made between such sinister apparitions and the benevolent souls of properly cared-for ancestors. In the popular way of speaking the former were called *kuei*, meaning demons, devils, and ghosts, while the latter were referred to as *shen*, meaning kindly spirits.

Now the material or *yin* component of the soul (called *p'o*) was that which would turn into a *kuei* if not placated by suitable burial and sacrifices. As for the burial, it was thought that this portion of the soul would reside in the grave as a natural habitat, both it and Earth being *yin*. If the deceased were properly interred and sacrificed to, the *p'o* soul would rest peacefully, while the spiritual or *yang* soul (called *hun*) would send down blessings to the surviving family members. This power of the *hun* soul derived from its nature as *shen*, which not only was a generic term for kindly spirits, but was used in reference to all deities.

Thus, the rites of burial and sacrifice were sanctioned both by fear of the dead becoming a vengeful demon, and by hope that the dead would become a benevolent god. Such a fear and such a hope underlie all of Chinese religion.

But we have not yet completed the Chinese theory of the soul. What has been sketched to this point is the native theory deriving from the remote past. At the the beginning of the Christian era the Indian religion of Buddhism had reached China, and within a couple of centuries enough of its texts had been translated into Chinese that new, imported notions of the afterlife began to influence Chinese concepts. These notions ultimately became inextricably entangled with the older Chinese ideas, particularly in the popular mind.

Although one of the Buddha's fundamental teachings was nonexistence of self—that is, of a "soul" in any permanent sense—common sense demanded some sort of continuing agent to carry out the process of karmic "justice." *Karma,* universally accepted in Indian religions including Buddhism, was originally an impersonal physical "law," comparable to the laws of action and reaction, or the conservation of energy. As popularly interpreted, however, it became a sort of merit and demerit system according to which the condition of one's future existence was determined by one's past actions. One reaped in the next life what one had sown in this. Furthermore, before being cast up by the wheel of life-death-rebirth into that next existence, one had to expiate in purgatory all of one's evil deeds. It is interesting that the most important social function of Buddhist monks in China was the priestly one of saying "soul masses" to alleviate as much as possible the sufferings of the soul in purgatory.

The chief value of these popular Buddhist notions was that they furnished incentive to do good and shun evil, while at the same time providing an explanation for the puzzling question as to why virtue was so often unrewarded and vice so frequently profitable—the answer in this case being that the books were always balanced although the figures had been written in the unknown ledger of a past existence. *Karma* required the soul as its agent, at least in minds unequipped to understand the higher Mahāyāna philosophy of Emptiness *(Śūnyatā)*, and so, by about A.D. 300, this soul had become an integral part of Chinese Buddhism.

During the later centuries, when Buddhism had spread all over China and was the strongest religious force in the land (its influence increased until the mid-ninth century, and was only seriously weakened by the rise of Neo-Confucianism in the Sung dynasty), these ideas about *karma*, rebirth, and purgatory were adopted into the folk religion. The end result was a purgatorial system organized along Confucian bureaucratic lines, with a well-organized program of karmic bookkeeping, trial in courts exactly like those of the magistrates in the Chinese empire, and punishment in various hells where the tortures meted out exactly fitted the crimes of the guilty souls. Those rare souls with an excess of good deeds over bad were of course able to pass directly into new births in favorable circumstances without undergoing these torments.

There were thus two theories of the soul, the first based on the *yin/kuei* and *yang/shen* concept of the native tradition, and the second based on the imported Indian belief in karmic process. The first is perhaps more closely bound up with the family religion and its ancestor worship, but the influence of the second is also very strong, especially in the funeral rites which are a vital part of the ancestral cult.

Man to Man. When the naturalistic world view of the Chinese was focused upon man as man, it found its subject of central interest. The nature of human nature

---

*Chinese Buddhism is discussed in Chapter 6. For more detailed treatment of Buddhism, see *The Buddhist Religion* by Richard H. Robinson in Dickenson's The Religious Life of Man series.

was always at the heart of Chinese philosophical discussion, with the result that ethics and social philosophy were more prominent than speculative thought. What it was to be a man, and what it was to be in various relationships with other men: these were the preoccupations of Chinese intellectuals through the ages. A few keen minds might wrestle with the abstruse problems of Buddhist philosophy, and many poetical minds turned to the pleasures of Taoist philosophy; but the main current was the humanistic rationalism of the Confucian School, which became the officially sanctioned doctrine in the mid-second century B.C.

As we shall see in Chapter 3, the religion of the family was the universal religious institution of China, and the ethical views of the Confucian tradition were essentially a rationalization and extension of the familial virtues. The principles of this familial morality were derived from natural relationships rather than abstract theory. By the early Chou dynasty the *Shu Ching* is referring to "the five classes," meaning fathers and mothers, eldest and younger brothers, and sons, and to the obligations of each "class." In *Meng Tzu* (see appendix), there is a somewhat different but similarly homely classification attributed by the philosopher Mencius (390–305 B.C.) to the times of the legendary sage-emperor Shun:

> Between father and son there is affection; between prince and minister there is integrity; between husband and wife there is a proper distance: between senior and junior there is proper precedence; between friend and friend there is faithfulness.[11]

And in the Confucian codes, *Li Chi* (see appendix), compiled in early Han (second century B.C.), yet a third form of the same domestic ethic is expressed:

> The father is merciful, the son filial; the elder brother is good, the younger brother submissive; the husband is upright, the wife complaisant; the adult is kind, the child obedient.[12]

This age-old familial morality, preached by Confucius and his principal followers and eventually enshrined in the Confucian Canon, came to permeate all of Chinese society. To the vast majority of the Chinese, who followed conventional careers, these precepts were the moral norm; to the minority who were different, it was this tradition from which they differed. Even Buddhist and Taoist monks and nuns, living apart from society, were still guided in their conduct largely by this Confucian family-style morality.

Above the level of the code of familial relationships was the body of ethical teachings meant for the "superior men," the small minority who received a literary education and who were thereby destined to govern the nation and to guide its cultural development. This higher tradition was directly inspired by the life and words of Confucius (551–479 B.C.). The Master exemplified the ideals by which all educated men should guide their conduct. He was a man to whom truth, honor, and the furtherance of just government meant everything. He stood for the good ways of the ancient sages. He sought all his life for a prince who would use him by putting his principles into practice; but when a ruler found expediency more profitable than principle Confucius left his service. Before Confucius, in

China as in old Europe, a "gentleman" was a man of noble blood; after Confucius, a gentleman was a man who possessed the *character* a gentleman should possess, regardless of his blood. This emphasis upon character, upon moral excellence, was the great contribution of Confucius to Chinese society.

The gentleman was to cultivate his own character, and, equally important, he was, like his Master, to put this highly cultivated character at the service of the State whenever this was feasible. The educated—those who mastered the Confucian Canon—served as officials, governing the untutored masses, a government that was in theory one of moral example rather than coercion. Confucius had said. "The Gentleman is like the wind; his inferiors are like grass. When the wind blows the grass must bend."[13] The full implication of this remarkable conception of government as moral example is seen in a passage near the beginning of the canonical *Ta Hsüeh* (*The Great Learning*—see appendix):

> The men of old who wished to make their bright virtue shine throughout the world first put in order their own states. In order to put in order their own states they first regulated their own families; in order to regulate their own families they first disciplined their own selves. In order to discipline their own selves they first rectified their own minds (or, hearts); in order to rectify their minds they first resolved sincerely upon their goals; in order to resolved sincerely upon their goals they first broadened their understanding of things to the utmost. The broadening of understanding to the utmost was accomplished by studying the nature of things.
>
> When they studied the nature of things then their understanding became complete; when their understanding was complete then they resolved sincerely upon their goals; when they were sincerely resolved upon their goals then their minds (or, hearts) were rectified. When their minds were rectified then they were able to discipline themselves; when they could discipline themselves then they could regulate their families; when they could regulate their families then they could put in order their own states; when their own states were in order then they could bring peace to the world.
>
> From the Son of Heaven (i.e., the emperor) down to the common people there is a single [principle]: discipline of the self is fundamental.

Thus, aside from their family religion, the educated elite in China had as their primary religious obligation the perfection of themselves to serve as moral paragons. The Confucian self-discipline was therefore quite different from the asceticism and yogic concentration of the Buddhist practice, or the breath-control, dietary, alchemical, and other techniques of religious Taoism (see Chapter 6).

Moral perfection was summed up in the term *jen* (pronounced like *run*), whose graph eloquently expresses its basic requirement: it is formed from the elements "man" and "two." From this composition of the word, translators have derived such renderings as "man-to-manness" and "human-heartedness," attempting to improve on older definitions such as "benevolence" or "goodness." There is actually no doubt that in common usage *jen* came to be no more than goodness or even just charity, but to Confucius it stood for such an exalted ideal that he had never known a person to whom the word could truly apply.

Aside from *jen,* the virtues stressed in the Confucian teachings are down to earth and easy to understand, or at least we can approximate them with the names of virtues familiar to Western morality: righteousness, loyalty, trustworthiness, modesty, frugality, incorruptibility, courtesy, learning, and the like. If they seem like moral platitudes it is because they were practical ideals in the education of gentlemen destined to run the empire. The important thing to understand is that it was this *concentration upon character-building* which engaged the minds of the men who governed China and created her high culture. It was this that engaged them, rather than other forms of the religious quest.

Finally we should note that in this naturalistic view of man there is no original sin, no inherent depravity from which man can only be lifted by a savior. There was, to be sure, a running debate throughout the history of Chinese philosophy as to whether human nature is good, bad, or morally neutral. But even those philosophers who proposed the second of these alternatives did not conceive of "badness" as a sort of taint, ineradicable except by divine grace. The majority view in the Confucian tradition was that given its authoritative expression by Mencius, who argued that human nature was inherently good. His greatest opponent was Hsün Tzu (340–245 B.C.), but Hsün Tzu merely insisted that men were inherently *inclined* towards evil and selfishness, and he believed that they would become good through education. The Confucian tradition subsequently blended these two views: the goodness of human nature was generally accepted in theory, while education was given the place of supreme importance in practice. In any case, there was no question of sinfulness and salvation in the Western sense.

SELECTED READINGS

Chan, Wing-tsit, *A Source Book in Chinese Philosophy.* Princeton, N.J.: Princeton University Press, 1963; papercover available. Generous selections in authoritative translations, with excellent introductions.

De Bary, W. T., *et al., Sources of Chinese Tradition.* New York: Columbia University Press, 1960; 2 vol. papercover available. Another widely used anthology.

Hughes, E. R., *Chinese Philosophy in Classical Times.* London: J. M. Dent & Sons, Ltd. New York: E. P. Dutton & Co., Inc., 1942. Superior translations with stimulating commentary.

Chai, Ch'u, with Winberg Chai, *The Story of Chinese Philosophy.* New York: Washington Square Press, 1961; papercover. Mostly on the Chou philosophers. Very brief, nontechnical, accurate, and interesting.

Fung, Yu-lan, *A Short History of Chinese Philosophy.* New York: The MacMillan Company, 1948; papercover available. Particularly good on neo-Taoism, Buddhism, and neo-Confucianism.

Needham, Joseph, *Science and Civilization in China.* Cambridge (England): Cambridge University Press, 1954 to date. A multi-volume work in progress. See especially vol.

II, *History of Scientific Thought,* 1956. This truly great work is one of the most impressive examinations ever undertaken of any civilization. Combines profound scholarship, brilliant creative imagination, and a distinguished literary style.

Thompson, Laurence G., *The Chinese Way in Religion.* Encino, Calif. and Belmont, Calif.: Dickenson Publishing Co., Inc., 1973. See Part One: The Ancient Native Tradition; Part Four, chap. 18: Most Holy Former Master, the Philosopher K'ung.

2.

Proto-Science and Animistic Religion

Regularity and Caprice in the Pre-Scientific World

It is not within the scope of this book to deal with complex questions of the origins of religion according to psychological and anthropological theories. However, we consider that the strangeness of the traditional religious life of the Chinese masses to the student in contemporary Western society requires at least a few suggestions concerning its milieu.

In our first chapter we became acquainted with the world view of the Chinese native tradition. This world view was mainly that of the elite educated class, as it was formulated in the texts of the Confucian Canon and by several of the great philosophers of the later Chou dynasty. When we come to consider the outlook of the Chinese people as a whole we find a rather different world view. It is not unrelated to the more sophisticated view of the intelligentsia, but it is more an animistic than a naturalistic one. In this popular world view the ancient tradition native to China was markedly influenced by the Buddhism imported from India, as we have already noted in our discussion of the theory of the soul. By way of background to the popular animism with its Buddhist admixture we shall make a few remarks regarding man's life in the prescientific world.

It is not easy for the Westerner living in a highly industrialized, scientifically progressive, technologically advanced civilization to visualize even how his grandfather lived only fifty years ago. Such is the accelerating rate of scientific-technological progress that nowadays there are greater changes between decades than formerly between centuries. But the first requirement for understanding the popular religion of China is the ability to enter into the spirit of a people whose lives and thoughts are as foreign to us today as those of our own medieval forebears. Like these, the great masses of the Chinese population were peasants, illiterate, unimaginably provincial in their experience, dwelling in tiny villages or small towns in the midst of their fields, largely out of contact with the high culture of the elite class, uncared for by the remote imperial government but always subject to taxation, corvée, and military conscription. Their masters were the landowner, the county magistrate, the local bandit chief. Living at all times on the very margin of subsistence, they had so few earthly possessions that we can scarcely conceive of such poverty.

For all their ignorance and confinement these peasants were wise in the ways of the seasons, skilled in the management of water, and unsurpassed in their mastery of tillage. And though they read no books they were thoroughly imbued with the Confucian ethic, which at least after the beginning of the Christian era became widely disseminated through proverbs and moral axioms, the tales of storytellers and the rustic stage, and the ancestral cult. In fact, the gulf between the peasant masses and the philosophers was not nearly so great as that between a laborer and an academic philosopher today. Chinese philosophy for the most part stayed in touch with the simple realities of life and nature rather than flying to the stratosphere of abstract speculation. Such concepts as *yin, yang* and *tao,* the five operational qualities, the "gestalt cosmology," and so forth, were not only comprehensible in their elementary form to the untutored peasant mind, but must actually have derived originally from the "nature-wisdom" of the peasant.

We have emphasized that an important part of this world view was the consciousness of *regularity in change.* But this comforting, sense-making regularity was far from perfect. The capriciousness of nature was also notorious, and to no one more than the peasant. On the one hand, so dependable were the seasonal changes that in north China the solar year could be divided into twenty-four periods of fifteen days each,[1] and the specific natural phenomena peculiar to each period would usually, in fact, occur exactly as charted in the calendar. On the other hand, all too often the seasonable rain would fail to arrive, or the frost would come too early. Despite the peasant's mastery of the techniques of agriculture, despite his indefatigable toil and his incredibly patient care, now and then he would be overwhelmed by some sudden catastrophe such as flood, drought, or plagues of insects.

Life itself was precarious in a way we can hardly realize. Death of the mother in childbirth was common, while death of infants was even more frequent. As recently as the 1920's a study of rural areas in central China revealed that "one-half of those born in China die before they are twenty-eight years of age."[2] No vaccinations or inoculations immunized people from such prevalent diseases as smallpox and typhoid. No antibacterial medications prevented infections from reaching lethal potency. No surgery removed the swollen appendix. No measures of hygiene and sanitation were understood that could have forestalled the frequent, widespread epidemics of cholera, malaria, or plague. The terror of disease lay not only in its customarily fatal outcome, but perhaps even more in the unpredictability with which it struck. It is the same terror with which we today think about cancer. But today we are confident, because of the past record of science, that the cause and cure for cancer and every other dread disease will be found, while in China there was no such history of progress upon which to base such a hope.

Conditions of this sort produce as a natural psychological defense an attitude of resignation to the inevitable. This resignation, often described as fatalism, has frequently been noted by Western observers, who were accustomed to reproach the Chinese for such a pessimistic and spiritless attitude. These observers forgot that only a few lifetimes ago their own ancestors required an equal amount of fatalism (expressed as resignation to the will of God) to bear up in a world of unpredictable disasters beyond human control. It is only the power acquired through science which has enabled man to become optimistic and actually successful in many of his encounters with the afflictions of nature. Modern man turns to science, confident that by choosing the correct application of scientific method any problem can be solved.

Prescientific man could have no such confidence, because prescientific methods had no history of increasing success. These methods resembled what we call science in that they were attempts to make sense out of the infinite multitude of facts in the universe, and that upon the theoretical bases thus constructed systems of practical application were erected. In China as in Europe these prescientific efforts could not attain the authority we today attribute to science, because in fact their *results* were undependable. No matter how logically coherent the prescientific theories might have been, when practically applied there were simply too many contradictory results. In other words, these systems were what we today call pseudo-sciences—although they were not of course "pseudo" to the men of their time. There was unquestionably a certain amount of empirical truth in these pseudo-sciences which kept alive their credibility; and to men who lived before scientific method had been perfected, they were one important means by which to cope with the environment. The Chinese pseudo-sciences were in a general way the counterparts of those familiar to us in Western history. Although they had their special Chinese features, the Western terms are indicative of their nature: astrology, chronomancy, physiognomy, and so on. Chinese medical theory was likewise pseudo-scientific, dominated by the *yin* and *yang* functions of the five operational qualities—the latter an interesting comparison to the four Aristotelean "humors" of premodern Western medicine.

The pseudo-sciences were an outgrowth of the naturalistic world view on the one hand and the animistic view on the other. The regularity in change of the first view furnished a basis for hypotheses of order in nature, while the conception of the world and all things in it as alive conditioned the particular nature of these hypotheses. In the Chinese folk religion the ordered aspect of nature faded somewhat into the background, so to speak, while the animistic aspect was more prominent. This is not surprising since the function of religion was to give support to men in coping with the problems resulting from the unpredictable and capricious aspects of the world, rather than to provide an intellectually satisfying cosmology. The simplest way to account for disorders was to picture them as the willful activities of beings. These beings were in the ingenuous folk mind very much like human beings, except that they dwelt in the unseen spiritual dimension and had superhuman powers.

In fact, the whole animistic system was but an extension of the ideas we have already examined in our section on the theory of the soul. The gods, even those who had the most efficacious power, were essentially the same as the *yang* soul —called *hun* and titled *shen* (deity), as we recall—of human ancestors. The demons or malignant beings were essentially the same as the *yin* soul—called *p'o* and titled *kuei* (ghost or devil)—which issued from an inauspiciously sited or neglected grave to wreak vengeance upon mortals. The ancestral religion, as we shall see in Chapter 3, stressed those acts that would obtain blessings from the *yang* soul, and appease the *yin* soul, of one's ancestors. Just so, in the wider contexts of the community or the whole nation, the animistic religion functioned to secure the blessings of the deities and appease or render harmless the demons.[3] Thus, man played his part in maintaining that order of nature of whose fundamental processes he was conscious, and thus he had at least some hope that he could by his actions improve his fate.

The pseudo-sciences, then, were attempts to read the meanings of certain sets of signs that human ingenuity had detected and arranged into logical sequences. When such meanings are directly related to present and future happenings in people's lives, then pseudo-science becomes a form of divination. This term is also used to refer to another technique that seeks to bring man into communication with the spiritual beings in the invisible dimension.

Divination

There are two major motivations in divination. The first is the desire to understand the operations of the natural and supernatural forces in the environment so that one's own actions may be in accord with them, thus producing favorable results. The second is the filial responsibility to keep in touch with deceased family members so that one may do whatever mortals can do to help them in the nether world. The first may be seen as a logical procedure in light of the native world view; the second results from acceptance of the Buddhist notions about the fate of the soul.

As for the particular techniques of divination practiced in China, we may say that they have been as varied as those found in other cultures. But whatever method was employed, there was no hard and fast line between consulting the deities and reading the invisible ink in the book of natural principles. The rationalistic wing of the intellectuals might scoff at crude notions of ghosts and gods, and hold to entirely naturalistic conceptions; and yet many of their ideas were from the vantage point of science no more valid than the very superstitions they derided. In this respect there is a close correspondence with premodern Europe, whose learned men likewise seem to us to have been almost comically deluded about the real workings of the universe. There is even a correspondence in the scholasticism of the Chinese philosophers with their colleagues in medieval Europe. The Neo-Confucian philosophers of the School of Natural Law (*li*), whose Thomas Aquinas was Chu Hsi of the twelfth century, spun elaborate webs of metaphysical and cosmological theory and even emphasized that one should search out the principles in things; but after all their searching was entirely speculative and lacked experimental and mathematical basis.

There is still a further parallel between these Chinese thinkers and the premodern Europeans: the latter could not find the road to true science because they were prisoners of tradition—their reverence for Aristotle, Galen, the Bible, and other ancient authorities constituted a mental block. In exactly the same way, the Chinese were victims of their reverence for ancient authorities. Although Buddhism had introduced various types of idealistic thought, yet the native naturalism prevailed. The most influential source of this naturalistic theory was the *Canon of Changes,* the *Yi* (or, *I*) *Ching.*

The Yi Ching. The *Yi* is one of the core works of the Confucian Cannon (see appendix), but it is no more the exclusive property of the Confucian literati than the concept of *tao* is the special possession of the Taoists. It is no doubt one of the most influential books ever written, no small part of its continuing, universal appeal being that it is so ambiguous and suggestive that every reader is challenged to find its true significance. Unfortunately, it will not be possible here to convey any adequate idea of its contents, which would involve us in lengthy technical discussions. We must be satisfied to indicate in a general way its place in the proto-scientific world view of the Chinese.

The *Yi Ching* evolves from eight trigrams consisting of all the possible combinations of broken and unbroken lines, placed one atop another:

The eight trigrams are further developed into sixty-four hexagrams by the simple method of putting one trigram on another and carrying out the same procedure to combine broken and unbroken lines in all possible combinations.

The unbroken line stands for *yang,* the broken line for *yin.* The diagrams are symbols as wholes, and each line is also a symbol. There grew up about each diagram a text to explicate its significance, line by line, and as a whole. It seems certain that the original work was a diviner's text. By casting lots the diviner determined whether the first line would be *yin* or *yang;* he then built up the diagram from bottom to top, casting lots for each line.

The oracular judgments on the diagrams are no doubt the heart of the *Yi Ching,* but at various unknown times during the Chou dynasty other sections were added to give us the present text. Tradition attributes these additions to ancient sages, including Confucius himself. It is these commentaries which have lifted the work from its original position as a fortune-telling manual to the status of a profound revelation about the principles of the cosmos. Unfortunately, as we have remarked, this philosophizing is so far from lucid that many of the most intelligent minds in Chinese history have failed to explain it satisfactorily. Nevertheless the symbolism of the diagrams became in the Chinese world the main system of conceptualization of the universe. In the prescientific attempt to formulate universal principles and grasp the operational modes of nature, the diagrams played a part comparable to that of mathematics in modern science. The diagrams were dynamic, in the sense that the arrangement of lines changed as one took different readings, and it was this changing which interested the Chinese mind. Hence the title of the book, indicative of the Chinese view that the cosmos was a functioning organism rather than a static object. Because the concern of Chinese scholars was predominantly with moral, social, and political problems, and not with the physical world as such, the content of the commentaries was bent to humanistic purposes. Nevertheless it supplied the humanistic philosophers with what seemed a sound metaphysical rationale.

Now the interesting thing, the thing we must grasp in order to appreciate the functional part played by the *Yi Ching* in Chinese religion, is that there was a subtle, vital shift in the attitude with which the diagrams were regarded. Originally they had been symbols—visual representations of what happened in given circumstances. But eventually they came to be invested with *operational power*. They no longer simply stood for specific changes, they actually brought about these changes. It was this belief which gave the *Yi Ching* its dominance in the Chinese world view and molded many of the elaborate, pseudo-scientific theories. The diagrams were key components in the complex system of correlations which underlay all this pseudo-science, and which involved the five operational qualities and many numerical constructs.[4]

Divination could be performed for any situation to relate it to any other situation by virtue of the fact that the diagrams were thus related to all the primary factors in the scheme of things. These primary factors included not only the operational quality dominant in the particular situation, but also the color, musical note, flavor, position of various heavenly bodies, compass point, season, and so forth, and so on.

Feng-shui. So far as religion is concerned, the most influential pseudo-science was that of "winds and water," the literal translation of *feng-shui.* This is usually called geomancy in Western writings, but we prefer the transliterated term because the Chinese pseudo-science does not correspond very well with any Western lore. *Feng-shui* constitutes a system of divination for determining the auspicious siting of human dwellings—for the living or for the dead. The rationale is that which we have already considered, namely, that man may help improve his own fate by determining the workings of nature and then bringing his own actions into accord with them. The theories of *feng-shui* purport to explain what the pertinent natural processes are, and the practices of *feng-shui* are designed to effect the desired results. Since we already know the basic premise that the spirits of the dead are very influential in the world of the living, it is unnecessary to explain why the siting of graves should be a crucial matter or why the homes of the living should be located in the most favorable situations.

We shall not be surprised to learn that the fundamental thing is to place the grave or home properly with regard to the functioning of *yin* and *yang.* The former is represented in the technical vocabulary of *feng-shui* as the white tiger and the latter is called the azure dragon—which in fact stand for the cardinal points of west and east. Eitel has summed up the basic theory as follows:

... The azure dragon must always be to the left, the white tiger to the right of any place supposed to contain a luck-bringing site. This therefore is the first business of the geomancer on looking out for a propitious site, to find a true dragon, and its complement the white tiger, both being discernible by certain elevations of the ground. Dragon and tiger are constantly compared with the lower and upper portion of a man's arm: in the bend of the arm the favourable site must be looked for. In other words, in the angle formed by dragon and tiger, in the very point where the two (magnetic) currents which they individually represent across each other, there may the luck-bringing site, the place for a tomb or dwelling, be found. I say it *may* be found there, because, besides the conjunction of dragon and tiger, there must be there also a tranquil harmony of all the heavenly and terrestrial elements which influence that particular spot, and which is to be determined by observing the compass and its indication of the numerical proportions, and by examining the direction of the water courses.[5]

The topographical characteristics of the earth are in themselves manifestations of the *yin* and *yang* forces that can be seen more obviously in meteorological phenomena, and which as wind, rain, clouds, clear-sky heat, and so forth, are quite fittingly designated as "breaths" (*ch'i*). But in the Chinese view the earth is no different from the heavens in pulsating with the breaths of the two primal forces:

Wherever there is nature's breath pulsating, there will be visible on earth some elevation of the ground. Where nature's breath is running through the crust of the earth, the veins and arteries, so to speak, will be traceable. But nature's breath contains a two-fold element, a male and female, positive and negative ... breath. ... Where there is a true dragon, there will be also a tiger, and the two will be traceable in the outlines of mountains or hills running in a tortuous and curved course. Moreover, there will be discernible the dragons's trunk and limbs, nay, even the very veins and arteries of his body, running off from the dragon's heart in the form of ridges or chains of hills. As a rule, therefore, there will be an accumulation of vital breath near the dragon's waist, whilst near the extremities of his body the energy of nature's breath is likely to be exhausted. ... But even near the dragon's heart, the breath of nature, unless well kept together by surrounding hills and mountains, will be scattered. When the frontage of any spot, though enjoying an abundance of vital breath, is broad and open on all sides, admitting the wind from all the four quarters, there the breath will be of no advantage, for the wind scatters it before it can do any good. Again, suppose there is a piece of ground with plenty of vital breath, and flanked by hills, which tend to retain the breath, yet the water courses near the place run off in straight and rapid course, there also the breath is scattered and wasted before it can serve any beneficial purposes. Only in places where the breath of nature is well kept together, being shut in to the right and left and having a drainage carrying off the water in a winding tortuous course, there are the best indications of permanent supply of vital breath being found there. Building a tomb or house in such a place will ensure prosperity, wealth and honour.[6]

From these remarks it will be understood why the entranceways to temples usually have at least slightly U-shaped walls, and why the tombs of southern

China are surrounded by horseshoe-shaped walls. For what nature has failed to provide, man may artificially correct.

Such artificial improvements of a situation are equally necessary to prevent the malign effects either of the topography itself, or of malicious spiritual beings:

> Now, all these evil influences, whether they be caused by straight lines of hills or water courses or by rocks and boulders, can be fended off or counteracted. The best means to keep off and absorb such noxious exhalations is to plant trees at the back of your abode and keep a tank or pond with a constant supply of fresh water in front of your house. This is the reason why in South China every village, every hamlet, every isolated house has a little grove of bamboos or trees behind and a pond in front. A pagoda, however, or a wooded hill, answers the same purpose. . . . Another device to keep off malign influences is to place opposite your house gate a shield or octagonal board with the emblems of the male and female principles, or the eight diagrams painted thereon, and to give the pathway leading up to your front door a curved, or tortuous direction. Lions carved in stone or dragons of burnt clay also answer the same purpose, and may be placed either in front of a building or on top of the roof; but by far the best and effective [*sic*] means is to engage a geomancer, to do what he says, and to pay him well.[7]

Why should the *yin* and *yang* be personified as they are in *feng-shui?* The answer to this question illustrates very well the correlative thinking of the Chinese pseudo-sciences. The system of correlations associated east with spring and west with autumn, as is quite appropriate in view of the symbolism of rising and setting sun. Spring, which brings all things to birth, is naturally *yang,* while autumn, portending the death of all things as seen most clearly in vegetation, is naturally *yin.* This correlation is but one of many which the *feng-shui* expert would make, and for which he used his elaborate compass.[8]

In the center of this compass is the needle which, like so many things Chinese, is viewed in reverse to our way of thinking—that is, it is seen as pointing south, rather than north. Surrounding the pit with its needle is a series of concentric circles, numbering from eighteen to twenty-four according to the completeness of the instrument. These circles contain the markings for all the various factors that must be considered in determining whether there is "a tranquil harmony of all the heavenly and terrestrial elements which influence that particular spot." Such factors include the eight trigrams, the cyclical signs called "heavenly stems" (*t'ien-kan*) and "earthly branches" (*ti-chih*),[9] stars, constellations, various arrangements of the five operational qualities, and others.

With so many factors to be correlated in addition to the visually determined aspects of the terrain, it is no wonder that often "the doctors differed." It was this wide leeway for interpretation afforded by all these calculations that kept alive the credibility of *feng-shui.*[10] If, despite the careful choosing of a spot for tomb or home, bad luck still visited the family, the obvious explanation was that the practitioner first consulted had not analyzed all the factors correctly—an explanation which the next expert would be sure to underline as he rectified the findings of his colleague.[11]

The Almanac. The principles given scriptural authority in the *Yi Ching,* and embodied in *feng-shui,* have been operative in all the pseudo-sciences. But one did not have to consult a specialist in order to know the trend of natural forces during the course of the year. In every home there would be found the almanac, which combined calendrical and cabalistic information in exactly the same manner as the almanacs frequently found in American homes only a generation or so ago. The publication of the calendar was from the most ancient times a distinctive prerogative of the Government; in fact, it was one of the symbols of the regime's legitimacy. It was issued in various versions, the contents of the cheapest being limited to the most essential information, while the most elaborate would be quite encyclopedic, forming a sort of popular manual for the household. Such an almanac, for the year designated by the combination of the "heavenly stem" called *jen* and the "earthly branch" called *ch'en,* that is, 1952, issued in Hong Kong, contains the following items, among many others:

> High and low tides for Kwangtung province; Taoist charms; the story of the encounter of Confucius with a precocious child; a list of the names of the "3,000" disciples of Confucius; the place-origins of Chinese surnames; a treatise on the analysis of dreams; fortune-telling methods (using physiognomy, palmistry, coins); the stories of the Twenty-four Paragons of Filiality; methods for cultivating longevity; the *Thousand-character Essay* (a sixth-century piece); the *Household Maxims* of the philosopher Chu Hsi; etc., etc.

All this material is copiously illustrated with wood-block cuts, and some of the printing is in two colors, red and black. But the essential information is that concerning divination, as based upon the astrological implications of the stems and branches, the five planets with their associated operational qualities, and the gods of certain stars. A "basic almanac" will give guidance as to actions that may be undertaken on each day of the year, while a fuller version such as the one here described will devote many separate sections to all the various aspects of divination, including the ruling natural forces, the connection of these with the forces ruling the life of a person born at any particular time, and the general and specific characteristics of every day and even every hour of each day.

For example, the following advice is given in one divinatory section of the Hong Kong almanac under discussion. On the twelfth day, denoted by the cyclical signs *hsin* and *ssu,* of the fifth month (that is, 4 June 1952)—a day under the influence of the operational quality of metal, and hence its associated planet, Venus—one should avoid mixing soya sauce, making liquor, or going on a journey. It is suitable, however, for getting together with friends, for taking up one's official duties, for marrying a wife or marrying out one's daughter, for making clothes, for moving, for treating an illness, for setting up the posts or raising the ridgepole of a house. . . .

If it seems that such mechanical or arbitrary divination could hardly command real belief, one need only consider that similar material is commonly found in bookshops and published in the newspapers of America today, and recall that many well-known personages in contemporary Western society are rumored not to take any important action without consulting their horoscope, in order to see the authority of this age-old, universal system lingering still in our scientific milieu. One can understand how much more pervasive and persuasive its influence would have been in the premodern age. The almanac thus shows us the eclectic character of popular Chinese religion, with its blend of naturalistic and supernaturalistic features.

Spirit Mediums. From the most ancient times the Chinese religion has utilized mediums for communicating with the spiritual realm. The medium is not like the gypsy woman with her crystal ball; he (or she) is rather the Chinese version of the shaman, who by certain techniques puts himself into a trance during which he is possessed by the spirit. The spirit may be that of any of the innumerable beings, eminent or humble, who inhabit the unseen dimension, and the medium speaks as the mouthpiece of this being. The spirit may be the chief deity of a temple who will give instructions to his followers, or it may be the soul of a person whose kinsmen want to contact him as he is undergoing the purgatorial interlude. The medium may be a professional, usually a young person having special gifts marking him for this career; or mediumship may be a temporary ability conferred upon a layman. The professional may be the star attraction of a temple, drawing to it crowds of people to seek the advice and help of the god, or he may have only a small private circle of clients. The medium may work matter of factly without any props at all, or as the popular performer in a big temple he may require special costumes, a sedan chair in which to be carried in procession with his god's image, weapons for inflicting self-torture and for expelling demons, musical stimulation, various attendants, an interpreter, and so forth. Sometimes the spirit speaks through the planchette, a technique analogous to the automatic writing of the West. Often the medium is given the power to speak in tongues, the most convincing demonstration of his true possession by the spirit being his ability to speak a dialect which in his normal state he does not even understand.

The medium, in his capacity of spokesman or representative of the deity, is naturally able to bless people by the power of the deity's spirit or to exorcise demons. The deity will give his power to an amulet, through the medium, who may cut his tongue and smear the charm with a bit of the blood. The medium of a temple may serve as medical advisor, psychologist, and business counselor to his clients as he relays to them the guidance of his familiar spirit. Some of the topics on which temple mediums in Singapore were consulted by Chinese clients, according to a field study undertaken in 1950–51, included the following, in order of frequency:

> "miscellaneous illness"
> "bad luck"
> possession by evil spirits
> erring spouses
> childbirth

investment advice
news of relatives in distant parts
the choice of auspicious dates
gambling advice
wayward children
accidents
advice concerning partnerships
insanity
protection in courts
communication with the dead[12]

The final item on this list is also a familiar service of mediums in the Western world. In China the communication may be for the purpose of comforting the dead or of receiving information and advice from them. An eyewitness account of a seance held for both of these purposes, a commonplace event in Hong Kong, is given by Burkhardt:

> Two sisters, employed as wash-amahs (laundry-women) in different houses in Hong Kong, wished to get in touch with the spirit of their deceased mother, who is buried in a village near Kukong, up the North River from Canton. The journey is expensive and tedious, and letters are few and far between. . . . A third sister is working in Singapore, but fails to answer letters. The idea was that a talk with the mother would clear up questions of the family welfare and solve the mystery of the sister's silence.
>
> The Colony has no lack of mediums, and the most unexpected women appear to be gifted in this way. A few are professionals, but the vast majority are amateurs who have no fixed fees, and give their services for "lucky money" a percentage of which is always returned. . . . The medium's only properties consist of a cigarette tin filled with rice and covered with a scrap of red paper, which acts as an incense burner. Having lit her three sticks, she clasps her hands above her head, intones a short prayer, and then seats herself in front of the improvised altar. Her clients sit alongside her on the sofa, and provide her with the data consisting of the name of the departed with whom communication is desired and the exact location of the grave.
>
> The medium closes her eyes, and joins her open hands with the finger tips touching and thumbs separate. This forms the "Eight directions," in one of which every spirit in the unverse is to be found. The first communication was startling, for the spirit replied that the mother was not available, as her father-in-law wished to speak with his grand-children instead. Being of the senior generation he naturally had precedence, and no objection could be raised to his monopolising the conversation. He first identified himself by giving an account of the family, which children had died, and how the others were employed. These details are always expected to ensure that the right spirit is at the other end of the line. Having established his identity, the grandfather declared that the family had decayed since his days and, that though not actually in want, his descendants were none of them prosperous. . . . He attributed the reduced circumstances of his descendants to the fact that a house had been built in front of the family mansion which had broken its luck. . . .*

*That is, blocking off the benign emanations deriving from a site with good *feng-shui.*

As to the correspondence with the girl in Singapore the old man stated that her letters were being stolen, and that they should write by registered post with receipt to sender. . . . On the termination of the conversation the old man was of course asked if he were in need of anything. He replied that he was well off for clothing, but could find a use for $500, and gave minute directions as to how it was to be sent. The mode of communication was through the "Third daughter-in-law" and "Fifth Princess" through whom the medium carries out all her transactions with the Spirit world. . . .

In sending these remittances it is usual to remember other dead members of the family at the same time, lest their spirits should feel resentment at being neglected. In this case the mother, with whom communication was first sought, would certainly be propitiated by a packet. Gifts are also included in the despatch on behalf of other living members of the family, who have not had the opportunity of hearing the request of the deceased. . . .

Of course the old gentleman's modest demand for a remittance of $500 was not taken at its face value and, when the time for despatch arrived packets of notes on the Bank of Hell, and quantities of white paper stamped with a golden square were purchased from the purveyor of underworld commodities. . . .

A lucky day, fifteenth after the conversation with the grandfather, was chosen for mailing the packet, and at noon the consigner presented herself with her parcels at the medium's hut . . . [which] consists of two rooms and a lean-to kitchen, scrupulously clean throughout. The bamboo table altar was backed by a watercolour of her Patron Saint, "The Third Daughter-in-law." . . .

The money to be despatched is placed on the altar accompanied by a quantity of cheap blank paper slips with rough holes punched in two rows lengthways. These represent the insurance, and are intended to distract malignant spirits who infest the route from interference with the packets. . . . The priestess after lighting three sticks of incense, places herself on the right of the altar and the client takes up her position on the left. After committing the packages to the safe keeping of the Saint, with a few short prayers to beseech her good offices, the money is enclosed in the pre-addressed envelopes. The officiant offers them one by one, igniting a corner of the envelope from the candles on the altar. They are then handed to the consigner who moves to the front of the altar and waves the blazing mass three times up and down, before carrying it to the door to be consumed in a brazier.

The whole ceremony only occupies about ten minutes and the participants have the same confidence in this mode of despatch as they have in the services of the General Post Office.[13]

Man Against Demons

The deities, or spiritual beings whom we have designated by the general term *shen,* represent the benignant influences constantly working on man from the unseen, but entirely real, spiritual dimension of the world. Since that dimension is in effect but a continuation of the visible world, evil must exist in it as well as good. We know already that the *shen* are the spiritual essences of the *yang* souls and that the *kuei,* or demons, are the spiritual essences of the *yin* souls. We also know that while the *yin* and *yang* theory originally had no moral connotation, and was only a way of conceptualizing the workings of the universe, in the popular way of thinking these terms when applied to souls took on the connotations of good and evil. The *shen* are honored, flattered, and asked for blessings; but the *kuei* are feared, guarded against, and propitiated.

While the Chinese perhaps invented nothing new in the real of demonology, they certainly developed the subject as extensively as any people on earth. Their *kuei* are of every conceivable variety and inhabit every environment. Animals, plants, insects, mountains, forests, and waters all harbor specters. They are at work in illness and suicide; they operate as vampires and vultures.

The broadest generalization covering the activities of malignant spirits is that it is they who are responsible for any untoward happening, any sort of trouble which cannot readily be explained by a more obvious cause. From nightmare to madness, from strange noises to ghostly apparitions, from melancholia to death by smallpox, from losses at gambling to the ruination of a once flourishing family, from tripping to drowning—the catalogue of devils' mischief is endless. Everyone was exposed to danger throughout every day of his life, although certain circumstances were especially favorable to the evil designs of these spirits. Women in childbirth and helpless infants were obviously vulnerable, as could be seen in their high mortality rate.

But it is especially significant that in the last analysis the depredations of malignant spirits were not a principle of evil working for its own ends, but were actually the instrument of *karma.* The *kuei* were after all maleficent because they had been wronged, either through improper burial or neglect, or in their mortal term. Their vengeful natures might cause them to harm those who apparently were innocent, but if one could know all the facts, one would find the karmic process working in the long run with perfect justice. Plenty of cases were known to everyone in which the work of evil spirits was quite apparently retributive justice. Some of these involved persons who had been driven to suicide by merciless creditors, mothers-in-law, or officials, and who in return drove their persecutors to confession, to ruin, to punishment by the law, or even to suicide on their own part.

Defense and Propitiation. Even though *karma* theoretically would work its way, of course nobody—innocent or guilty—would passively submit to the attacks of its agents in the form of evil spirits. Precautions against attack took many forms, a few of which have already been mentioned in our discussion of *feng-shui.* Charms and amulets were universally employed, placed in the home and worn on the person.[14] Guardian figures were painted on the gates, and walls were placed across the entranceways beyond, in both temples and homes, to keep out evil spirits. Small children, particularly the all-important males, would be called by derogatory names by their parents in order to fool the demons into thinking that they were of so little value that it was no use to attack them. The spiritual power of a *shen* was a potent antidote to the baleful influence of the *kuei,* and there were many household gods which served this purpose.

Just as the common man stood in awe of the literati officials, so the common run of specters would not dare to bother these powerful personages, and those things which gave them this power—notably the books and other furnishings of the scholar's study—were in themselves talismans against the evil ones. In China, as elsewhere, the surest safeguard against the malicious power of demons was the purity of a moral life bolstered by deep learning and true faith in religion. The power of the literati derived in actuality from their knowledge of books, and this "knowledge," like the Western knowledge of the Bible, was above all knowledge of the true Way. Needless to say, the more strictly religious character of the Buddhist and Taoist priests gave them in the popular mind much power against the devils. The Taoists especially were professionally qualified as demon-fighters, and would be employed to write charms, to drive evil spirits out of the home with incantations and sword-waving, and to exorcise the demons who possessed men's bodies and souls.*

The *yin* spirits might also be propitiated and not simply warded off. It was recognized that many of them were more to be pitied than censured, particularly those who were categorized as "hungry ghosts"; that is, those whose plight was simply that they had no sacrifices from their descendants. One of the most widely observed festivals in the yearly religious calendar was that which took place on the fifteenth day (full moon) of the seventh month, called the "*kuei* festival," or, as it has been largely taken over by Buddhism, the *Yü-lan hui,* often described in English as All Souls' Day. During the entire seventh month the gates of Hades were open so that the hungry ghosts might roam about; they returned to their gloomy abode on the last day of the month, which is the birthday of their special savior, the Chinese Bodhisattva Ti-tsang. The *kuei* festival was marked by many observances intended to comfort the neglected spirits and to ensure that their resentment would not bring misfortune to the living. Services were held in all Buddhist temples and many private homes. Offerings were set out, incense was burned, families tended to the tidying up of their own tombs, and "Hades money" and many other paper items for the use of the spirits were sent across in conflagrations. In many places paper boats with paper crews were set afire and sent out on lakes, rivers, or the sea. Nor were the bereaved spirits neglected in the official religion, for every local seat of government was furnished with a special altar dedicated to them.†

Exorcism. Exorcism means the driving out of *kuei.* Its success is dependent upon the triumph of *yang* over *yin,* and many individual features of exorcist rituals will be recognized as deriving their efficacy from their *yang* nature. In the following description, taken from Burkhardt, we have marked obvious *yang* symbols by asterisks:

*These magical functions of the clergy may be traced back to the magicians (*fang-shih*) of late Chou times (see Chapter 6).

†We have written in the past tense, but it is to be noted that in this, as in so many other features of the folk religion, the beliefs and practices of the past linger on today.

A special altar is arranged on which are burning candles* and incense sticks.* In many countries peach wood* is believed to possess mystic qualities . . . so the exorcist is provided with a sword of that material, or the demon-dispelling weapon formed by welding copper cash coins* into a tapering line. This was also hung above the bed of a person suffering from nightmares. The priest places it upon the altar and prepares a scroll on which talismanic inscriptions* are penned. The officiant reverently burns the charm and mingles the ashes with a cup of pure water* from the spring. With the sword* in his right hand, and the cup in his left he prays for power. "Gods* of Heaven and Earth, invest me with the healing seal that I may purge this dwelling of all evil lurking therein!" Having received his mandate, he invokes the demons. "As quick as lightning, begone." He then picks up a sprig of willow* which he dips in the cup, and sprinkles first the east, then west, north and south corners of the house. To re-enforce the spell he fills his mouth with the water, and spurts it against the east wall with the invocation* "Slay the azure spirits of the east, spawn of unlucky stars, or let them be expelled to a distant country." The red demons of the south, the white in the west, and the yellow in the centre, are similarly banished to the accompaniment of gongs* and crackers* whose efficacy is commensurate with the riot of sound they create. When the pandemonium is at its height, the exorcist raises his voice to be heard above the din and screams: "Evil spirits of the East get you back to the East, of the South return thither. Let all demons seek their proper quarters and vanish forthwith." The officiant then makes his way, sword in hand, to the door and goes through the exercises to preclude all chances of return.

Exorcists are not tied down to a set form of ritual, and vary their methods to suit their clientele. Sometimes the doorposts are sprinkled with the blood and feathers of a freshly killed cock,* and a single demon may be disposed of by fixing a padlock round his neck. . . .[15]

The most dramatic scene in the entire picture of man's warfare with the malignant spirits is the attempt to cast out devils that have taken over a human being. Demon-possession is a very ancient and universal phenomenon, on which the last word has not yet been said. Whatever scientific explanation psychiatry may eventually be able to provide, such possession has seemed an undeniable fact to countless witnesses up to the present day. For those who might assume that demon-possession and exorcism are only fairy tales from the past, it may be something of a shock to read an eyewitness account from the autobiographical book by Peter Goullart published in 1961:

We arrived at a medium-sized stone courtyard, half-way up the hill, situated in front of a temple. There was a small group of onlookers standing in corners in the shadow of the wall, among them a distracted couple who . . . were the energumen's parents. The energumen himself, a rather emaciated man of about twenty-five . . . lay on an iron bedstead on a rush mat. He was very pale and there was a wild, roving look in his fevered eyes. The [Taoist] priest . . . was attired in full ritual robes and stood before a portable altar on which was an incense burner, the small image of a god, a vase with holy water, a ritual sword and other articles and a book from which he was reading. Two monks were assisting him, whilst four muscular men watched the prostrate demoniac.

The abbott was reading the scriptures in a monotonous, droning voice, repeating *mantras* [spells] over and over again with a great deal of concentration. Then he stopped and, taking an elongated ivory tablet, the symbol of wisdom and authority, he held it ceremonially in both hands in front of his chest and approached the bed slowly. There was a visible transformation on the energumen's face. His eyes were filled with malice as he watched the priest's measured advance with a sly cunning and hatred. Suddenly he gave a bestial whoop and jumped up in his bed, the four attendants rushing to hold him.

"No! No! You cannot drive us out. We were two against one. Our power is greater than yours." The sentences poured out of the energumen's distorted mouth in a strange, shrill voice, which sounded mechanical, inhuman—as if pronounced by a parrot. The priest looked at the victim intensely, gathering all his inner strength; beads of perspiration appeared on his thin face.

"Come out! Come out! I command you to come out!" He was repeating in a strong metallic voice with great force. "I am using the power of the One compared to whom you are nothing. In His name I command you to come out." Immobile, he continued to focus his powers on the energumen's face. The man was struggling in the bed with incredible strength against the four men who held him. Animal growls and howls issued from time to time from his mouth which became square, his teeth gleaming like the fangs of a dog. . . . I had the impression that a pack of wild animals was fighting inside his body. . . . Terrible threats poured out of the contorted mouth, now fringed in white foam, and interspersed with such incredible obscenities that women had to plug their ears with their fingers. . . .

Again the abbott cried his command to the unseen adversaries to leave the prostrate man. There was a burst of horrible laughter from the victim's throat and suddenly with a mighty heave of his supernaturally strengthened arms he threw off the men who held him and jumped at the priest's throat like a mad bloodhound. But he was over-powered again. This time they bound him with ropes and fastened the ends to the bedposts. . . . The abbott, still immobile, continued his conjurations in a metallic voice, his eyes never leaving the body. With unutterable horror, we saw that it began to swell visibly. On and on the dreadful process continued until he became a grotesque balloon of a man.

"Leave him! Leave him!" cried the monk concentrating still harder. . . . Convulsion shook the monstrous, swollen body. . . . It seemed that all the apertures of the body were opened by the unseen powers hiding in it and streams of malodorous excreta and effluvia flowed on to the ground in incredible profusion. . . . For an hour this continued and then the energumen, resuming his normal size, seemed to come to rest, with his eyes watching the unmoved priest who was still reading. . . .

The priest stopped reading; with sweat pouring down his face, he backed down to the altar, laid down the tablet and took up the ritual sword. Threateningly and commandingly he stood again over the energumen.

"The struggle is useless!" he cried. "Leave him! Leave him in the name of the Supreme Power who never meant you to steal this man's body!" Another scene of horror evolved itself before our dazed eyes. The man on the bed became rigid and his muscles seemed to contract turning him into a figure of stone. Slowly, very slowly, the iron bedstead, as if impelled by an enormous weight, caved in, its middle touching the ground. The attendants seized the inert man by his feet and arms. The weight was such that none of them could lift him up and they asked for assistance from the onlookers. Seven men could hardly lift him for he was heavy as a cast-iron statue. Suddenly he became light again and they put him on a wooden bed which had been brought in. A long time passed with the abbott reading and commanding interminably. At last he sprinkled the inert man with holy water and advanced to him again with a sword. His concentration was so deep that he did not seem to see anybody. He was utterly exhausted and swayed slightly. Two novices came up to support him.

"I have won!" he cried triumphantly in a strange voice. "Get out! Get out!" The energumen stirred and fell into dreadful convulsions. His eyes rolled up and only the whites were visible. His breathing was stertorous and he clawed his body until he was covered with blood. Foam was issuing from his mouth and a loud gurgling sound.
. . .

"Damn you! Damn you!" came a wild scream from the foaming lips. "We are going but you shall pay for it with your life." There was a terrific struggle on the bed, the poor man twisting and rolling like a mortally-wounded snake and his colour changing all the time. Suddenly he fell flat on his back and was still. His eyes opened. His gaze was normal and he saw his parents who now came forward.

"My parents!" he cried weakly. "Where am I?" He was very feeble and they carried him out in a specially ordered sedan chair. The abbott himself was in a terrible state of prostration and was half-carried and half-dragged away by his novices. . . .[16]

Those who will credit the veracity of this account will be prepared to believe, as Mr. Goullart did, the statement of his Taoist hosts that these exorcist priests sacrificed years of their mortal lives as the price for every victory of this kind, their vital forces drained and spent. We may believe this, regardless of what explanation we can think of for the phenomenon of demon-possession itself.

SELECTED READINGS

Forke, Alfred, *The World-Conception of the Chinese.* London: Arthur Probsthain, 1925. Useful, although not completely reliable.

Burkhardt, V. R., *Chinese Creeds and Customs,* 3 vols. Hong Kong: South China Morning Post, Ltd., 1953–58. Personal observations among Chinese in Hong Kong and vicinity, with charming illustrations by the author.

Elliott, Alan J. A., *Chinese Spirit Medium Cults in Singapore.* London: London School of Economics and Political Science, Department of Anthropology, 1955. Report of field study by anthropologist.

Lessa, William A., *Chinese Body Divination.* Los Angeles, United World Academy and Fellowship, 1968. Comprehensive and copiously illustrated study by anthropologist.

Freedman, Maurice, "Geomancy," *Proceedings of the Royal Anthropological Institute of Great Britain and Ireland for 1968,* pp. 5–15. Presidential address, 1968; includes comprehensive bibliography.

Wilhelm, Hellmut, *Change: Eight Lectures on the I Ching.* New York: Pantheon Books, Inc., published for the Bollingen Foundation, 1960; papercover available. The only lucid discussion of the subject by an authority.

March, Andrew L., "An Appreciation of Chinese Geomancy," *Journal of Asian Studies,* Vol. XXVII, No. 2, 1968, pp. 253–268. Brief, well-written discussion of the basic theories, by a geographer.

Jordan, David K., *Gods, Ghosts, and Ancestors: the Folk Religion of a Taiwanese Village.* Berkeley, Los Angeles, and London: University of California Press, 1972. See Chapter 4 on divination. From field report by anthropologist.

3.
The Family: Kindred and Ancestors

Central Importance of the Ancestral Cult in Chinese Culture

The central importance of the family is no doubt the specific distinguishing characteristic of Chinese society; and the function of the ancestral cult is certainly the specific distinguishing characteristic of the Chinese family. The family is of course important in Western religion, with its sacrament of marriage, its commandment to honor the parents, and its duty to raise the children in the true faith. But the religious character of the Chinese family goes far beyond these aspects. This character, developing out of the so-called ancestor worship, makes religion in China more a family matter than an indivudual choice. *Family religion is basic, while individual and communal religion are secondary.* For this reason we shall consider the former now and place the latter at the end of our study.

Ancestor worship is not restricted to the Chinese, but whereas it has usually been considered a feature of primitive cultures, in China it has been the very warp of a high culture throughout millennia of time. There is evidence of the centrality of the family cult as far back as archeological findings take us, in the Shang or Yin dynasty before 1000 B.C. Such findings include tombs with a rich content of artifacts, the foundations of royal palaces, and much else. History, meaning the evidence given by written documents, starts with this material, in the form of inscribed bronze ritual vessels and oracle bones. It is these oracle bones which show us most clearly how the religious system of the most ancient age was based on ancestor worship.

The oracle bones were instruments of divination. The diviner smoothed off the surface of tortoise shell or cattle scapula and bored into this surface a series of concave depressions. He then scratched onto this prepared surface a question the king wished to put to the supernatural powers. Touching a red-hot poker to the cavity beside the inscribed question, the diviner produced cracks in the bone, which he then interpreted as the response. The answer was noted down, and confirmation that the answer had been correct was often added later by way of maintaining the credibility of the oracle.

These bones with their writing have been of the utmost value to historians in revealing some facets of the ancient culture. But the question that particularly concerns us is the identity of the "supernatural powers" to whom the questions were addressed. In the words of Tung Tso-pin, the leading authority on the subject, "The one hundred thousand pieces of oracle bones and shells contain little but the questions the reverential Yin kings put to their ancestors and the answers in the form of cracks. . . ."[1] Tung concluded, after more than thirty years of study of these bones and shells and all the other archeological evidence, that despite their other religious beliefs "it was still ancestor-worship that held the most important position in the religious life of the Yin people. 'To serve the dead as if they were living'—we can say that the piety of the Yin people did reach that degree."[2] And again, "almost all the elaborate religious rituals of the Yin dynasty were meant for the ancestors."[3]

Thus, we see that the basic importance of ancestor worship in Chinese religion, upon which all modern observers have agreed, has been characteristic since the most remote past. But ancestor worship is not merely the ritual observance of individuals. It is rather the root from which grows the trunk of the lineage tree with its many family branches. In order to grasp the meaning of ancestor worship we shall need to understand the lineage and family system to which it has given rise.

The Lineage and Its Families as a Religious Corporation

The Chinese word we have rendered as lineage is *tsu. Tsu* refers to the male descendants of a common ancestor, bearing the same surname, and including their wives and children.* Because in the course of several generations this will become a very large group, the *tsu* will naturally separate into sub-lineages and their constituent families who may live in the same vicinity or spread apart according to circumstances.

Since the *tsu* is patrilinear, the families of wives are excluded. A woman marries into her husband's lineage, and her relationship with her father's lineage becomes minimal. Since ancient times the countryside of China has been dotted with villages, with a market town or city here and there. Many of these villages, even today, are in fact lineage villages whose families live in separate compounds but close together. Brides for the village's boys are obtained from neighboring villages, or perhaps from one particular village, while the girls are in turn sent to those villages in marriage. The term for the woman's lineage is "outside-*tsu*" or "outside relatives."

The marked difference between the Chinese and Western systems is thus the vital role of the lineage in the former. Whereas in the West the nuclear families typically split off from the patrilinear stem, which was therefore biologically but not socially senior, in China the families typically remained attached to their lineage, and organically parts of a larger functioning whole. The lineage with its families might be either more or less cohesive, depending upon various economic and social factors. But in any case the reality of the lineage corporation was

*We ignore the complexities of the subject and give the simplest possible definition. One should be aware, however, that historically many changes have taken place in the family system, and that there are innumerable local variations on the system and its religious components.

effectively symbolized by the religious cult of the common ancestors—particularly the founding ancestor.

The origins of this corporation are lost in antiquity, but in the ritual codes written several centuries B.C. we have the detailed outline of its structure and functioning. This structure places each individual in a specified position with regard to all others according to generation and collateral distance. These relative positions are not only indicated by kinship terms, but are strikingly exemplified in the degrees of mourning. The closer the relationship, the more the ceremonial grief required. Thus, for example, a man wore the coarsest sackcloth for the longest time (nominally three years, but actually somewhat over two) in mourning for his parents, as did a wife for her husband and her husband's parents; while a less primitive dress would be worn for only nine months for such relatives as a married aunt, a first cousin, or (by a wife) for her husband's grandparents.

The elaborate mourning rites and the wearing of mourning garments for long periods of time served to renew the lineage ties, especially when life expectancy was short and deaths in an average *tsu* were frequent. Furthermore, the ultimate reunion of the kinsmen in the ancestral temple served to confirm lineage solidarity. The ancestral temple was the home of the tablets inhabited by the spirits of all the lineage's deceased members. Here the souls of the ancestors were visibly personified in the rows of wooden tablets standing in order according to their respective generations and relationships on shelves under the tablet of the High Ancestor of the lineage. Periodically all available members of the lineage would assemble in the temple to celebrate their communal sacrifices to their forebears. Genealogical records, kept sometimes for many centuries, as well as "family instructions" written by leading personalities, were additional instruments for maintaining the in-group feeling of the lineage.[4] Finally, the Chinese State reinforced the institution of the *tsu* and its constituent families by leaving in the hands of its elders all governmental authority except that unavoidably the responsibility of the state, and by backing up with criminal law (*fa*) the family-lineage prescriptions for proper conduct (*li*). It is to these *li* that we now turn for further understanding of the religious character of the Chinese family.

Religious and Ethical Functions of Li

The word *li* is of broad connotation, extending from the most weighty religious ceremonies to the trivialities of daily etiquette. It means the norm of human behavior in all social circumstances. The ideograph with which it is written is composed of two parts, a signific indicating communication with the supernatural, and an additional element which is originally a pictograph of a sacrificial vessel containing some object. There could hardly be a more explicit indication of the religious basis for proper social behavior. We know little of the *li* of the Shang or Yin age, but from the succeeding Chou dynasty we have voluminous records. In the earlier centuries of the period the aristocratic rulers of the feudal states were apparently governed by an elaborate code resembling the chivalric codes of the European knights. At every court there were officials whose expert knowledge of the code was essential to the rulers. Confucius himself (551–479 B.C.) was an authority on *li,* and the school that developed to spread his teachings laid great stress upon this subject.

The *li* were not originally of universal application, for in the society of Chou China there was a sharp distinction between nobility and commoners. Just as in feudal Europe, the former supposedly behaved in accordance with the unwritten principles of *noblesse oblige,* while the latter were subject to harsh punishments. In the Chinese phrase, the *li* did not extend to the commoners, and punishments did not extend to the nobles. But as the feudal system disintegrated during the latter half of Chou and gave way to what was in effect a system of rival, independent states, the political conditions produced a social mobility unfavorable to the survival of an aristocratic caste. By the Han dynasty, in the second century B.C., when the polity was finally established in its imperial form, we may say there was a general extension of both *li* and *fa:* much of the former became accepted throughout the Chinese society, while the abolition of the hereditary nobility meant the applicability of the criminal law to all persons with little distinction. (In later times the new aristocracy of the literati held a privileged position in law, but they could at any time be reduced to commoner status for due cause.)

In the appendix on the Confucian Canon will be found a brief description of the works dealing specifically with *li.* Like the Torah of Judaism, these writings on the one hand represent the compilers' understanding of the ways of the ancients, and on the other have served as the living law for all subsequent generations.[5] If to modern eyes much of this material is incredibly hair-splitting, we must remember that it is our age which is exceptional in its freedom of thought and behavior. In any case, there was a sound rationale in the background of these codes:

> They are the rules of propriety [li] that furnish the means of determining (the observances towards) relatives, as near and remote; of settling points which may cause suspicion or doubt; of distinguishing where there should be agreement, and where difference; and of making clear what is right and what is wrong. ... To cultivate one's person and fulfil one's words is called good conduct. When the conduct is (thus) ordered, and the words are accordant with the (right) course, we have the substance of the rules of propriety. ...
>
> The parrot can speak, and yet is nothing more than a bird; the ape can speak, and yet is nothing more than a beast. Here now is a man who observes no rules of propriety; is not his heart that of a beast? ... Therefore, when the sages arose, they framed the rules of propriety in order to teach men, and cause them, by their possession of them, to make a distinction between themselves and brutes.[6]

The profound influence of *li* as seen by the codifiers is clearly set forth in the following:

> In the right government of a state, the Rules of Propriety serve the same purpose as the steelyard in determining what is light and what is heavy; or as the carpenter's

line in determining what is crooked and what is straight. . . . When a superior man (conducts the government of his state) with a discriminating attention to these rules, he cannot be imposed on by traitors and imposters.

Hence he who has an exalted idea of the rules, and guides his conduct by them, is called by us a mannerly gentleman, and he who has no such exalted idea and does not guide his conduct by the rules, is called by us one of the unmannerly people. These rules (set forth) the way of reverence and courtesy; and therefore when the services in the ancestral temple are performed according to them, there is reverence; when they are observed in the court, the noble and the mean have their proper positions; when the family is regulated by them, there is affection between father and son, and harmony among brothers; and when they are honoured in the country districts and villages, there is the proper order between old and young. . . .[7]

The functional purpose of the *li* so well expressed in these passages is fully borne out in the numberless rules actually found in the code: that is to say, in functional terms they serve primarily to demarcate the senior from the junior, the superior from the inferior. Whether it was the social system in the large, or the small but complete system of the *tsu* and its families, the underlying principle was hierarchical. This was so whether the *li* dealt with the religious or the secular aspect:

> The son of Heaven [the king] sacrifices (or presents oblations) to Heaven and Earth; to the (spirits presiding over the) four quarters; to (the spirits of) the hills and rivers; and offers the five sacrifices of the house,—all in the course of the year. The feudal princes present oblations, each to (the spirit presiding over) his own quarter; to (the spirits of) its hills and rivers; and offer the five sacrifices of the house,—all in the course of the year. Great officers present the oblations of the five sacrifices of the house,—all in the course of the year. (Other) officers present oblations to their ancestors.[8]

On a less exalted plane:

> He who pares a melon for the son of Heaven should divide it into four parts and then into eight, and cover them with a napkin of fine linen. For the ruler of a state, he should divide it into four parts, and cover them with a coarse napkin. To a great officer he should (present the four parts) uncovered. An inferior officer should receive it (simply) with the stalk cut away. A common man will deal with it with his teeth.[9]

Although the feudal order, in which such rules were the most effective means of reiterating rank, disappeared after Chou times, the spirit and even much of the substance of the codes continued in effect. Anyone with experience of social life among the Chinese today will recognize the following pattern of courtesy:

> Whenever (a host has received and) is entering with a guest, at every door he should give place to him. When the guest arrives at the innermost door (or that leading to the feast-room) the host will ask to be allowed to enter first and arrange the mats. Having done this, he will come out to receive the guest, who will refuse firmly (to enter first). The host having made a low bow to him, they will enter (together). When they have entered the door, the host moves to the right, and the

guest to the left, the former going to the steps on the east, and the latter to those on the west. If the guest be of the lower rank, he goes to the steps of the host (as if to follow him up them). The host firmly declines this, and he returns to the other steps on the west. They then offer to each other the precedence in going up, but the host commences first, followed (immediately) by the other. They bring their feet together on every step, thus ascending by successive paces. He who ascends by the steps on the east should move his right foot first, and the other at the western steps his left foot. . . .[10]

Recognizing that the *li* served as the means of emphasizing status in the society, we may ask the further question as to why such a system should have been developed in the first place, and once developed, why it was successful—that is, accepted by the society for ages. As in every society the whole code of behavior rested upon an ideal. The ideal in China was called *hsiao,* which is commonly rendered as filial piety. As with other fundamental concepts of a culture, simple translation cannot fill out the rich range of meanings in this term, and we must study it in some detail.

Hsiao: The Motivating Ideal

The written symbol for *hsiao* (filiality) is as clear in its significance as the ideograph for *li:* it consists of the graph for old, supported by the graph for son placed underneath. There could be no simpler nor yet more adequate summary of the ideal of *hsiao.* In amplification we may adduce a few of the countless statements on the subject to be found in the pages of the Confucian Canon.

From the sayings of Confucius himself: In reply to a question as to what *hsiao* is, "The Master said, 'While [the parents] are living, serve them with *li;* when they die, bury them with *li;* sacrifice to them with *li.*"[11] From the sayings of Mencius, the authority second only to Confucius: "Mencius said, 'Which is the greatest duty? Duty to parents is the greatest. . . . Among our many duties, the duty of serving the parents is fundamental. . . .'"[12]

From the *Hsiao Ching* (see appendix), a work which puts into the mouth of Confucius a systematic discussion of the subject, a famous passage:

> The Master said, "Filiality is the root of virtue, and that from which civilization derives. . . . The body, the hair and skin are received from our parents, and we dare not injure them: this is the beginning of filiality. [We should] establish ourselves in the practice of the true Way, making a name for ourselves for future generations, and thereby bringing glory to our parents: this is the end of filiality. Filiality begins with the serving of our parents, continues with the serving of our prince, and is completed with the establishing of own character."[13]

Again, from the same work:

> The Master said, "In serving his parents the filial son is as reverent as possible to them while they are living. In taking care of them he does so with all possible joy; when they are sick he is extremely anxious about them; when he buries them he is

stricken with grief; when he sacrifices to them he does so with the utmost solemnity. These five [duties] being discharged in full measure, then he has been able [truly] to serve his parents."[14]

And still again: "There are three thousand [offenses] meriting the five punishments, but there is no crime greater than unfiliality."[15] Lest this be thought to be merely a rhetorical statement, we mention the fact that unfilial conduct was a serious crime under the law. It was a right of parents to put an unfilial child to death, or at least to denounce him to the authorities for punishment prescribed in the criminal statutes. Cursing one's parents was a capital offense. We may understand the full implications of *hsiao* by noting what sorts of behavior were indictable:

> The grounds for such an accusation were the prosecution or cursing of one's grandparents or parents; not living with grandparents or parents and separating one's property from theirs; failure to support one's grandparents or parents; marrying, entertaining, or ceasing to observe mourning before the end of the required mourning period; concealing a parent's death; and falsely announcing a grandparent's or parent's death. . . . However, if a parent prosecuted a child as unfilial on other grounds, the authorities would not reject the case for this reason.[16]

Hsiao is thus the basis of the family's government, the cardinal virtue of the good man, and the most powerful force operating to maintain the orderliness of society required by the State. Now let us see what *hsiao* meant in practice.

Marriage is in all cultures rationalized as an institution for the production and nurturing of children. But whereas we tend to think of this in terms of the future of mankind—or at least the future of our own line—the Chinese tended to think of it as the most important requirement *for the support of the older generation and the generations that had already passed away.* The duty of Chinese children was theoretically to devote themselves without reservation to the welfare of their parents. The duty of a son's wife was to share in this complete devotion to her husband's parents. The personal feelings of the son and his wife were hardly taken into account. The codes of *li* contained explicit instructions:

> [Sons and sons' wives] should go to their parents and parents-in-law [on the first crowing of the cock]. On getting to where they are, with bated breath and gentle voice, they should ask if their clothes are (too) warm or (too) cold, whether they are ill or pained, or uncomfortable in any part; and if so, they should proceed reverently to stroke and scratch the place. They should in the same way, going before or following after, help and support their parents in quitting or entering (the apartment). In bringing in the basin for them to wash, the younger will carry the stand and the elder the water; they will beg to be allowed to pour out the water, and when the washing is concluded, they will hand the towel. They will ask whether they want anything, and then respectfully bring it. All this they will do with an appearance of pleasure to make their parents feel at ease. . . .
>
> While the parents are both alive, at their regular meals, morning and evening, the (oldest) son and his wife will encourage them to eat everything, and what is left after all, they will themselves eat. . . .

No daughter-in-law, without being told to go to her own apartment, should venture to withdraw from that (of her parents-in-law). Whatever she is about to do, she should ask leave from them. A son and his wife should have no private goods, nor animals, nor vessels; they should not presume to borrow from, or give anything to, another person. If any one give the wife an article of food or dress, a piece of cloth or silk, a handkerchief for her girdle, an iris or orchid, she should receive and offer it to her parents-in-law. If they accept it, she will be glad as if she were receiving it afresh. If they return it to her, she should decline it, and if they do not allow her to do so, she will take it as if it were a second gift, and lay it by to wait till they may want it. . . .[17]

Thus, the son and his wife were required to live with his parents, owed absolute obedience to them, and had no independent property rights. Chinese literature is full of edifying stories about filial sons and daughters and daughters-in-law who were reputed actually to have sacrificed everything for the comfort and well-being of their parents, according to such ideals.

Marriage, far from being primarily a union of man and woman to satisfy their personal desires, was primarily a family matter, as is shown in the fact that the bride was chosen by the son's parents and usually would never have been seen by him before the wedding. Everything about the betrothal and wedding, including the religious sanctions, was calculated to reinforce the subordination of the young couple to the bridgroom's family—especially his parents. For example, the expensive presents given to the bride's family emphasized that she was in fact being purchased by the boy's parents for their son. The matching of horoscopes and the traditional belief that marriages were "made in heaven" lent an air of inevitability to decisions that actually were made on hardheaded business or "political" grounds by parents and go-betweens (the latter essential in this, as in many other social relations). Formal worship of the bridegroom's ancestors brought the bride under the supernatural authority of his forebears and reminded her that her membership in her natal lineage was terminated. She was now a probationer, so to speak, among the kinsmen of her husband—and both of them were economically dependent upon his parents. Only by earning the respect, or at least the tolerance, of the parents, could the new wife really gain security in her role; thus filial conduct towards her in-laws was literally a matter of life and death. The children of this union were likewise regarded as essential to completion of the couple's filial responsibilities, as is indicated by a saying of Mencius which became proverbial: "There are three ways in which one may be unfilial, of which the worst is to have to no heir."[18]

Not to have an heir was a heinous offense against *hsiao* because without such an heir the ancestral sacrifices would be discontinued. In the event that the wife should not, in fact, produce a son, an acceptable substitute would be found either by making the son of a concubine the heir or by adopting a son from some close branch of the *tsu*. Where there was more than one son, the eldest was charged with the responsibilities of the ancestral cult. In feudal times the aristocracy followed the rule of primogeniture, and so firmly did the special position of the

Top, country wedding: the bride is carried in her red-covered sedan chair to the home of the groom's family, with dowry preceding her. *Bottom,* old and new in a Taiwanese country wedding: Western wedding gown and Western suit are popular, but a sieve with the *t'ai-chi,* or symbol of cosmic unity, is held over the bride's head, a very old custom designed to insure blessings upon her.

eldest son become settled in the Chinese society of ancient times that even the disappearance of the feudal system and the establishment of a more equalized inheritance law did not radically change it.

Destined as he was to replace his father as head of the family and to be invested with the solemn duties of principal sacrificiant to the ancestors, the eldest son was from childhood set above his younger brothers. They owed him, in fact, almost the same obedience and respect that they owed the father himself, since the latter's authority would eventually pass to him. The same principle, when applied more broadly to the *tsu,* gave the eldest son of the direct line the same sort of status among all the males of his generation:

> Eldest [male] cousins in the legitimate line of descent and their brothers should do reverent service to the son, who is the representative chief of the family and his wife. Though they may be richer and higher in official rank than he, they should not presume to enter his house with (the demonstrations of) their wealth and dignity. . . .
>
> A wealthy cousin should prepare two victims, and present the better of them to his chief. He and his wife should together, after self-purification, reverently assist at his sacrifice in the ancestral temple. When the business of that is over, they may venture to offer their own private sacrifice.[19]

We are now in a position to appreciate why the rites of mourning and the sacrifices to the ancestors are the fundamental manifestation of the Chinese religion, embodying as they do the sacred character of the lineage and its families as a kinship corporation. The great principle of *hsiao* which should govern the lives of all its members was expressed in formal modes of behavior systematized as *li,* and the culminating acts of *li* were those of ancestor worship.

The Theory of Ancestor Worship

Meaning of the Term. Let us recognize at the outset that the expression "ancestor worship" is much disputed in its connotations and hence unsatisfactory. The word "worship" should not mislead us into supposing that there is a generally accepted interpretation of the real purport of these *li* comprising the ritual services to the ancestors. As early as the seventeenth century this question arose among the Catholic missionaries who had to decide whether or not their converts would be allowed to continue the practices concerned. The question took this form: Are these rites truly religious or are they less than that, something like respectful memorials?

It was far from being an academic question. Indeed it took on the proportions of a major doctrinal dispute, known in history as the "Rites Controversy," involving popes and Chinese emperors and leading eventually to the downfall of the Jesuit position in China and expulsion of all missionaries from Chinese soil. The problem was never resolved, and to this day there is no agreement on the interpretation of the rites—which suggests that the question may have been wrongly put in the first place. It is, in fact, a question that could only have arisen in the Western mind, which is accustomed to placing the family, the individual, and religion into separate categories. In addition to this inappropriate categorizing, there is the difficulty that Western definitions of "religion" itself are conflicting and disputed. We propose therefore to avoid dealing with such a question at all, and it is to be understood that we use the term "ancestor worship" as a matter of convenience.

The first point to understand about ancestor worship is that it is confined to the kinship group. As Confucius said, "Sacrifice to spirits which are not those of one's own dead is [mere] flattery."[20] Ancestor worship thereby played an indispensable role in reinforcing the cohesion of family and lineage. It should also be pointed out that this kinship group strength was achieved at the price of divisive effects in Chinese society as a whole. The ancestral cult was the one universal religious institution, but by ensuring the exclusiveness of each *tsu* it fastened on the nation a system of closely knit in-group units, each of which claimed the major share of each individual's loyalties and efforts at the expense of a larger social consciousness.

There were certain underlying assumptions in the ancestral cult. Obviously such a cult assumed continuance of personality in some form after death of the physical body. It further assumed the possibility of continued contact between dead and living family members. Finally, in the light of the family system and its hierarchical structure, it was assumed that original relationships remained in full force despite the death of a senior. In fact, because of the mysteriousness of their post-mortem condition the deceased seniors were conceived to possess even more spiritual power than they had possessed in life. The love and fear of the son for the father were perhaps increased by the latter's continuing presence in spiritual rather than physical form.

The ancestors were thus in a sense deified. *This conception of deification of the ancestors ultimately colored all of the Chinese religion, which may be seen as an extension of this idea.*

Status of the Ancestors. In order to understand the status of the ancestors we may turn in the first place to the earliest literary records, dating from the first centuries of the Chou dynasty. In *Shu Ching* (*Canon of Historical Documents*) and *Shih Ching* (*Canon of Poems* or *Songs*), the ancestors of the ruling house are pictured as dwelling "on high" in some sort of close association with, and subordinate capacity to, the Supreme Ruler in Heaven. Their power over their descendants seems to derive from this position; that is, they are able to intercede with *shang ti* or *t'ien* to send down blessings or calamities:

> . . . It is not that the former kings do not aid us later men, but the king is dissolute and tyrannical and thereby makes an end to himself. Therefore Heaven rejects us. . . .[21]
> The scribe then put on tablets the prayer, saying: Your chief descendant So-and-So [the king's name would be tabu] has met with an epidemic sickness and is violently ill. If you three kings [referring to the ancestors immediately preceding the currently

reigning king] really . . . owe a great son to Heaven (i.e. if he must die), then substitute me, Tan, for So-and-So's person. . . .[22]

Many sections of *Shu Ching* have been aptly described as political propaganda, in which the Chou rulers are attempting to persuade the descendants of their former overlords, the Shang or Yin kings, that they should acquiesce in the new regime. A couple of passages from such sections will illustrate the assumption that the spiritual world is but another dimension of the temporal world, the two being in intimate association:

> Anciently our former kings together with your grandfathers and fathers . . . shared ease and toil. . . . Now when I offer the great sacrifices to the former kings, your ancestors follow and together with them enjoy them. . . .[23]

> Anciently our former rulers toiled for your grandfathers and fathers. If you have injurious intents in your hearts, our former rulers will . . . restrain your grandfathers and fathers (so that) your grandfathers and fathers will reject you and not save you from death.[24]

Mutual Dependence of Dead and Living. From those most ancient times the assumption was that living and dead were dependent upon each other, the latter for sacrifices and the former for blessings. In *Shih Ching* we have preserved to us some vivid pictures of the transaction between the two parties which took place in the ancestral temple:

> Ah, the glorious ancestors—
> Endless their blessings,
> Boundless their gifts are extended;
> To you, too, they needs must reach.
> We have brought them clear wine;
> They will give victory.
> Here, too, is soup well seasoned,
> Well prepared, well mixed.
> Because we come in silence,
> Setting all quarrels aside,
> They make safe for us a ripe old age,
> We shall reach the withered cheek, we shall go on and on.
> With our leather-bound naves, our bronze-clad yokes,
> With eight bells a-jangle
> We come to make offering.
> The charge put upon us is vast and mighty,
> From heaven dropped our prosperity,
> Good harvests, great abundance.
> They come [the ancestors], they accept,
> They send down blessings numberless.
> They regard the paddy-offerings, the offerings of first-fruits
> That T'ang's descendant brings.[25]

The relationship of mutual dependence, with its expectation of tangible blessings in exchange for filial nourishment, may be said to describe the common attitude of Chinese down to the present. A proper ceremonial funeral, burial in a grave auspiciously located according to the principles of *feng-shui* (see Chapter 2), the spirit-tablet reverently set up and regularly given homage, and the more formal sacrifices on special occasions—for these demonstrations of the continuing love and remembrance of their descendants the ancestors would send down to them the sorts of things any parents would wish for their children: good luck, health, happiness, official position, wealth, sons, love of virtue, long life, and a peaceful death.

Significance of the Rites in the Eyes of Confucian Scholars. Although such an ingenuous view was held by the great masses of simple people—and we need to keep in mind that in all ages the Chinese populace has consisted largely of illiterate peasants—there was a more sophisticated interpretation. The educated elite tended toward a less literal, or more cautious, or even completely rationalistic belief:

> Sacrifice [or, He sacrificed] as if (the deceased) were present; sacrifice [or, he sacrificed] to the spirits as if the spirits were present.[26]

The problem in this passage is the sense in which "as if" is to be taken. It might mean "as if—although in fact they are not"; or it might mean "as if—assuming that they actually are present even though unseen."

> The Master did not discuss strange phenomena, feats of strength, disorders, or spirits.[27]

Although we are told here that Confucius did not discuss spirits, we are not told *why* this was so, and the answer to this question is not necessarily that he did not believe in them.

> Chi Lu asked about serving the souls of the dead. The Master said, "Not being able [adequately] to serve [living] men, how can we serve the souls of the dead?" [The disciple then said,] "I venture to ask about death." [The Master] said, "Not yet knowing [?what we ought to know] about life, how can we know about death?"[28]

This famous utterance has usually been taken to indicate a *disinterest* in the supernatural, an interpretation which is surely borne out in the rest of the *Analects.* The Confucius of this record is concerned with man and not with the realm of the spiritual. On the other hand, to jump from this to the conclusion (as so many have done) that Confucius was "agnostic" is just as certainly wrong. The same work gives us many statements of the Master referring to Heaven, to the power of Heaven, and even to Heaven's protection and sponsorship of Confucius himself. Confucius was regarded by later generations as the final authority on *li,* and the *Analects* furnishes proof that he took the ancestral rites very seriously.

The explicit rationalizing of the rites of the ancestral cult was the work especially of the philosopher Hsün Tzu (340–245 B.C.), whose interpretations found their way into *Li Chi.* According to his view:

> The emotions produced in him who performs sacrifice by his memories, ideas, thoughts, and longings, cause him to change countenance and pant; it cannot be that

such feelings should never come to him. . . . If such feelings come in vain, then the emotions produced by his memories and ideas are disappointed and not satisfied, and that which the rite (*Li*) could have satisfied is lacking. For this reason the early Kings established ceremonies for the purpose of honouring the honoured and loving the beloved to the utmost. Hence I say: Sacrifice is because of the emotions produced by memories, ideas, thoughts, and longings; it is the extreme of loyalty, faithfulness, love and reverence; it is the greatest thing of the rites . . . and of beautiful actions. . . . The Sage plainly understands it; the scholar and superior man accordingly perform it; the official observes it; among the people it becomes an established custom. Among superior men it is considered to be a human practice [Tao]; among the common people it is considered to be serving the spirits.[29]

It is easy to see how it was possible for those who wished to understand ancestor worship as merely "reverence" and not "worship" to find firm ground for their interpretation in the authority of Confucian texts themselves. But if we reconsider the last sentence in the paragraph quoted, we note that the philosopher expresses a clear and significant distinction: "Among superior men it is considered to be a human practice . . . among the common people it is considered to be serving the spirits." How few, after all, are the superior men, and how greatly are they outnumbered by the common people, especially in a premodern, peasant society. An adequate description of Chinese religion must include not only the outlook of the small percentage of superior men, but the more naïve beliefs of the masses.

The Practices of Ancestor Worship

From the formal point of view ancestor worship may be divided into (1) the funeral rites, (2) the mourning observances, and (3) the continuing sacrifices to the *manes.* From the functional point of view these practices serve to express the grief of the survivors in accepted or ceremonial manner; to help the spirit of the dead in its progress through purgatory; to give peace to the *p'o* (*yin*) soul in the grave and forestall its becoming a malevolent ghost; to obtain the blessings of the *hun* (*yang,* hence *shen*) soul for the family, to give the family and clan a continuing sense of wholeness; and, of course, to demonstrate the love and remembrance —whether real or affected—in which the family continues to hold its deceased members.

Although there are innumerable local variations in the practices involved, they are still only variations on the same themes. Here, as in every aspect of Chinese culture, there is an essential unity despite superficial diversities. Every province, county, and even smaller unit in China will have its voluminous accounts of the local customs prevailing from ancient times, while the reports of foreign observers in various parts of China are likewise rich in details; but after all the underlying theories are the same, based upon the *li* texts of the Confucian Canon or the Buddhist notions discussed in Chapter 2.

Funeral Rites. It would be desirable to describe in detail the funeral rites, and to set forth their rich symbolism in all its complexity. Nothing would better convey the significance of the family religion in Chinese culture upon which we have insisted. Far from being an isolated event in the lives of the family members, a harrowing experience best gotten over as quickly as is decently possible so that the family life may get back to normal, the funeral and the subsequent mourning are protracted, momentous, and integrally a part of the normal flow of that family life. Properly performed, they assure the comfort and well-being of the deceased in his spiritual existence, and consequently the good fortune of his descendants. The funeral rites are, in fact, the binding force that holds together the family and the clan as a religious corporation through the generations.

Unfortunately, the space available to us does not permit even an outline of these rites, so we must be content to summarize their most essential features.[30] This summary is based upon accounts of the actual practices of the present day in one Chinese province, the island of Formosa, which the Chinese call Taiwan. Keeping in mind the introductory remarks made above, we may say that these Taiwanese practices are representative, *mutatis mutandis,* of what is done in other parts of China.

Longevity is one of the blessings most devoutly hoped for by the Chinese, and longevity is the standard euphemism used in the funeral when referring to death. For example, the graveclothes are called "longevity clothes." One begins to prepare oneself for death by getting ready such garments when one reaches the age of about fifty. A stout coffin and even a tomb, favorably sited according to *feng-shui* theory, are also a comfort to an old person, who is thus assured of the well-being of his soul.

One who is dying is placed upon boards supported on trestles and covered with a mat, in the main room of the home. The icons of the deities enshrined at the altar in this room are now covered to avoid contamination by the evil influences—something which is indeed guarded against at every step of the rites.

When life has departed, the corpse is washed and garbed in the graveclothes. In this, as in everything else connected with the funeral, the "filial son"—that is, the eldest son (with his wife)—plays the leading role. Now he seats himself outside the house wearing a "coolie hat" with a bamboo fillet into which are inserted two small red candles. His seat is a bamboo stool set upon a winnowing basket. He holds his arms outstretched with a piece of hemp rope across his shoulders, and the graveclothes are put on him, inside out. He is fed with "longevity noodles." The graveclothes are then transferred from the filial son to the corpse. It is worth noting that the graveclothes themselves are in the style of the Han dynasty (206 B.C.-A.D. 221), an example of the profound conservatism of this family religion.

All the family let their hair go unkempt, don sackcloth, and keep up a ritual wailing during specified times. The outside-family arrives to condole and takes part in the ceremonies. The mourning garments and the announcement cards are white, the color of death. What is not white is red, the color of life, and hence good fortune. Thus, these two colors symbolize the two themes of fear-propitiation

Top, funeral service: Buddhist monks chanting, mourners kneeling before spirit table and photograph of the deceased. *Middle,* articles thought to be needed by the deceased are sent across to the ethereal realm by burning. *Bottom,* visiting the tomb on Ch'ing-ming.

and hope-supplication, which run through the funeral rites and indeed through all Chinese religion, as has been pointed out.

The *hun,* or *yang* soul, upon which rest the hopes of the survivors and to which they address their supplications, is to reside permanently in a wooden spirit tablet on the altar in the home. Even before the soul is formally installed in this tablet it must be given a temporary resting place, which is called the "soul-silk." This is actually a paper object about a foot high and three inches wide, in the shape of a blunt sword, on which are written the tabu name of the deceased and certain other particulars. It is placed before the corpse to receive the prayers of the family, is later carried in the elaborate funeral procession, and is finally borne home from the grave by the eldest grandson. Once back in the main room of the home it is placed upon a small table which serves as a temporary altar. There also is placed an incense brazier which holds a bit of earth from the grave. Incense is kept burning continuously and the soul-silk receives the solicitous service of the filial son and other family members, as well as Buddhist and Taoist priests. Eventually, after the time has arrived to install the permanent spirit tablet, the soul-silk is carefully disposed of by burning. Now the spirit tablet is placed upon the altar beside the other ancestral tablets, while a pinch of the ashes from the brazier that stood before the soul-silk is put into the braziers of these other tablets. This is the final act of the funeral rites, and is appropriately called "joining the braziers," symbolizing, of course, the unity of all the ancestors, and hence of the family and lineage.

Every act of the funeral rites is performed in accordance with the prescriptions set forth in the ancient codes of *li.* But there is one conspicuous addition of later times: the participation of Buddhist and Taoist priests. The greater the financial means of the family, the more of these professional priests will be engaged and the more frequently they will hold their services. Following the death these services continue for seven weeks, which is a Buddhist innovation, and priests must be called in as often as possible. They perform on certain instruments, chant *sūtra,* and pray for quick passage of the soul through purgatory (the so-called "soul masses"). Some of these services last from noon to midnight, while others may begin one morning and go on until the third morning.

The funeral of poor people may be concluded within one to three days, but the wealthier the family the longer will the burial be delayed. During this period of delay the coffin remains in the main room, where it is constantly oiled to make it more waterproof and airtight while its inmate receives ritual sacrifice and wailing. In many cases, the burial of the coffin does not mark the end of the affair. It is followed within some years by what is called the "lucky burial." This involves exhuming the bones, washing, drying, and sunning them, and then storing them in a "golden peck-measure"—that is, an earthenware jar about three feet high and one foot in diameter. Following an indefinite period of storage, the jar and its contents are finally buried in a spot selected as especially auspicious by a *feng shui* augur.

Mourning. In our discussion of the lineage and its families as a religious corporation we pointed out that relationships were clearly exemplified by the degrees of mourning. This in itself is sufficient to show how much more important, how much more formalized, mourning was in China than in the West. Entirely aside from the normal human manifestations of grief, these ceremonial mourning practices served to reaffirm the family's internal cohesion and its status structure and to demonstrate to the outside society its virtue. Far from being an individual-istic expression of feeling, the mourning was regulated by detailed instructions set forth in the *li* scriptures, sanctioned by public opinion, and enforced if necessary by the law.

Five degrees of mourning were established. We shall illustrate the mourning practices by a brief quotation from *Yi Li (Ceremonial and Ritual;* see appendix) on the prescriptions for the deepest mourning:

The Three Years' Untrimmed Mourning.

> This mourning dress consists of an untrimmed sackcloth coat and skirt, fillets of the female nettle hemp, a staff, a twisted girdle, a hat whose hat-string is of cord, and rush shoes.
>
> The principal mourner lives in a booth built of branches leant against the house. He sleeps on straw and pillows his head on a clod.
>
> He wails day and night, with no set times.
>
> For food he sups up congee, made twice a day, morning and evening, with one handful of grain.
>
> He does not put off the head or waist fillet when he sleeps.
>
> After the sacrifices of repose, he cuts a hole in the side of the booth and fits lintel and door-posts to it. He lays a mat over the straw, and sleeps on this. For food he eats coarse rice, and has water for his drinking. He wails once in the morning and once at night only.
>
> When he assumes the raw-silk hat, at the end of the first year of mourning, he lodges in a structure called the "outer sleeping apartment," and eats for the first time vegetables and fruit, partaking also of his ordinary food. No definite times are then prescribed for his wailing.[31]

Such mourning was observed for the father, for the Son of Heaven by the feudal lords of Chou times, by a father for his heir, and by an adopted heir for certain family members.

There are many passages in the canonical texts in which the mourning practices are rationalized. We cite only one, showing the attitude of Confucius himself toward the three-year mourning:

> Tsai Wo asked about the three-year mourning, [his opinion being that] one year was already long enough. "If the True Gentlemen do not for three years carry on the practices of *li*, then *li* will certainly be harmed by this; if for three years they do not perform music, then music will certainly be lost. [In the space of a year] the old crops of grain are already no more, and the new grain has come up. . . . After one year [the mourning] might be ended."
>
> The Master said, "To eat fine rice, and to wear brocaded silk—would you feel comfortable doing [these things after one year]?"

[Tsai Wo] said, "I would."

The Master said, "If you would feel comfortable, then do them. But the True Gentleman, while in mourning, cannot relish the taste of his food, cannot enjoy the sound of music, cannot feel comfortable in his place—therefore he does not do [these things]. Now if you would feel comfortable, then do them."

When Tsai Wo had left the Master said, "Yü (Tsai Wo's personal name) is really heartless. Only after a child is three years old does it leave its parents' arms; and [thus it is that] the three-year mourning is observed everywhere under Heaven. Didn't Yü [himself] have the three-year love of his parents?"[32]

As we have said, these as well as other of the *li* passed from the monopoly of the nobility into widespread observance among the people as a whole following the end of the feudal age (about 200 B C). Nevertheless there were great discrepancies among the classes with regard to the strictness and elaborateness of their conformity to the ideal. The complete abandonment of one's daily duties prescribed for the eldest son was hardly practicable for a peasant family struggling to survive from year to year. Sumptuary laws also provided gradations in the required and allowed observances according to social class.

Nevertheless, among those able to follow them, the *li* were in force. The elite scholar class, as the avowed upholders of the Confucian principles, were especially the conservators of these practices. A minister of state engaged in work of great importance to the government must yet retire from office upon the death of his parent and observe the three-year mourning. Neglect of this filial duty would not only be considered disgraceful, but would be punished by law. Of all the *li,* however, the mourning rites have suffered most curtailment with the changing conditions of contemporary times. Modern life simply does not allow extended withdrawal from society by survivors, least of all the new head of a family.

Continuing Sacrifices to the Manes. Sacrifices are an aspect of Chinese religion most easily traced to the remote past. The burial of a king or other great personage was accompanied in Shang or Yin times by many sacrifices, whose remains have in recent decades been uncovered by archeologists. The great royal tombs at Anyang in the Honan province, last capital of that dynasty, contained both animal and human sacrifices, in addition to the bronze vessels and oracle bones already mentioned. The quantities of other goods accompanying the deceased to the grave indicate that the Shang kings were thought to require in their spiritual existence the same sorts of things they had needed during their mortal span. This theory took hold and was expanded to the populace as a whole, and in post-Han times was combined with the imported Buddhist notions we have already discussed.

The blending of the native and Buddhist theories means that sacrifices are in part a special function of the professional priests and in part the responsibility of the family and lineage heads. There is no need for any special consecration of the latter to such a function; their sacrifices to the ancestors are after all simply a continuation of the filial duties required of the son during the parents' lifetime. On the other hand, the effectiveness of these sacrifices marking such vital occasions as the mortuary rites would be substantially increased by the mysterious spiritual power commonly attributed to those who have been ordained in any religion.

The ancestors dwelt in three specific places: within the home, within the family or lineage cemetery, and within the lineage temple. As we know, the *yang* soul resided in the spirit tablet enshrined on the altar. Its presence in the company of the icons of other gods worshipped by the family further emphasized the deified status of the ancestor. Before the ancestral tablets, as before the other gods, were set the sacrificial implements—candles, incense, flowers, wine, and food. Not only was the head of the household supposed to see to it that these sacrificial offerings were renewed constantly, but whenever any event of importance occurred in the family the particulars were announced to the spirits in the tablets. Thus, the continued presence of the ancestors was made tangible to the family in their daily lives.

In the cemeteries owned by lineages able to afford them the tombs of the ancestors would theoretically be arranged in a manner that would indicate their positions within the kinship system. On several occasions during the year, as specified in the calendar of religious festivals, the family would visit the cemetery, see that the tombs were in good condition, and offer sacrifices and prayers. The cemetery and the grave were thus intimately a part of the family's sphere of interest and activity, rather than objects of dread designed to segregate the dead from the living. The old people in the family not only received the special respect of the young, but would often, as we have seen, be comforted by the acquisition during their lifetimes of graveclothes and coffins. A son who would provide such things in advance, for the peace of mind of his parents, was especially filial. This extended even to preparation of the tomb while the parent was still in good health. Among the peasant masses the expense of a cemetery was of course prohibitive; hence, the graves of the ancestors would be scattered here and there on untillable patches of land lying amidst the fields—a circumstance which, however, emphasized even more the closeness of past and present generations.

The factor of expense also limited possession of a lineage temple to the economically prosperous. Those which had the means would purchase land, erect a temple, and appoint lineage members as caretakers. At the periodical gatherings in this temple there would be accomplished the formal sacrifices to the ancestors, the communal feasting that renewed the kinship ties, the setting in order of genealogical records, and the settling of any business concerning the whole lineage by conference of its chiefs. The central fact of such gatherings is of course that everything was said and done in the presence of the ancestors, who not only sanctioned the decisions of the family and lineage heads, but who also shared in the pleasure of their descendants as they enjoyed themselves and felt the reality of their attachment with the group.

Keeping Their Glory and Their Teachings Alive. Finally, in such strong lineages, aside from the spirit tablets, the tombs, the ancestral temple, and all the religious rites associated with them, the memory of the ancestors was kept alive though the frequent recalling of their names and deeds. Genealogical accounts were maintained, often for many generations, and the young were taught reverence for their forebears. Some lineages treasured documents from the distant past in which eminent ancestors had laid down precepts for their descendants. Americans who are proud to be able to trace their ancestry back to colonial days may be astounded by the pedigrees recorded in the Chinese lineage books:

> Our family tree owes its existence to a sprout of a royal family planted in consequence of a feud somewhere in the lower Yellow River Valley some three thousand years ago. . . . My first ancestor in the Chiang line was made the first feudal lord to rule over that land toward the end of the twelfth century B.C. . . .
> From our first ancestor down to the present day all the names in the direct line have been recorded in our genealogy. How authentic they are I cannot tell, for their lives were so obscure that verification is not wasy. . . .[33]

> On the New Year's Eve of my twelfth year . . . my father called me into his study and sent me to ask my grandfather whether I might be shown the family clan book. . . .
> It was a memorable evening. All the lanterns in the hall were lit and my father, after changing his dress and burning incense at the ancestral shrine, climbed up a ladder and took down very respectfully the wooden case in which the clan books were kept. There were thirty or forty volumes. . . .
> Father . . . raised his voice and made a gesture of respect when the first name appeared. "This," he said, "so far as the records show, was our first ancestor." He did not speak the name, "Hsu," because it is not customary in China for a person to address or speak of an elder by name; he called him "Yuan-ching Kung." Yuan-ching was another name of our first ancestor, and Kung a respectful term used in referring to elders. . . . "Yuan-ching Kung lived," continued Father, "at the end of the first century B.C. and was appointed by the Emperor Ai government-inspector and Governor of Yen Chou." . . . The rule he made for his family is printed in large characters in the clan book. It consists of only four words: "Benevolence," "Righteousness," "Sincerity," and "Endurance." He commanded that each member of the family should be trained in these four qualities.[34]

The most eminent family in China is that of Confucius himself. The ancestral home in Ch'üfu, Shantung provice, has been preserved through the centuries as a shrine. The seventy-seventh lineal descendant, Mr. K'ung, Te-ch'eng, presently lives in Taiwan as a refugee from Communism. He holds the title of Duke, the only hereditary patent of nobility still extant (it was conferred in 1233). Appropriately enough, Mr. K'ung has several honorary positions of importance in connection with the preservation of the traditional Chinese culture and is in great demand throughout East Asia as a lecturer on Confucianism.

The connection of all this with the ancestral cult is evident. The careful maintenance of the genealogies* and the indoctrination of the children with the glorious traditions of their forebears help to keep the religious sentiment alive, and they reinforce the lineage and family solidarity in the most vivid way. This may serve as a touchstone for the vitality of the ancestral religion on which the whole structure of Chinese society and culture has been raised.

SELECTED READINGS

Yang, C. K., *Religion in Chinese Society.* Berkeley and Los Angeles: University of California Press, 1961; papercover available. Excellent analysis of the subject.

Groot, J. J. M. de, *The Religious System of China.* Leiden: E. J. Brill, 1892–1910. Reprinted in Taipei by Literature House, 1964, 6 vols. Family religion as seen in the mortuary rites is presented in great detail in the first three volumes.

Liu, Hui-chen Wang, "An Analysis of Chinese Clan Rules: Confucian Theories in Action," in Arthur F. Wright, ed., *Confucianism in Action.* Stanford, Calif.: Stanford University Press, 1959. Reprinted in same editor's *Confucianism and Chinese Civilization,* New York: Atheneum Publishers, 1964 (papercover).

Gamble, Sidney D., *North China Villages.* Berkeley and Los Angeles: University of California Press, 1963. An actual clan (i.e. lineage) history is discussed on pp. 239–262.

Chiang, Yee, *A Chinese Childhood.* New York: W. W. Norton & Co., 1963, papercover. Charming reminiscences with illustrations by the author. What it was like to grow up in a wealthy lineage-family environment.

Thompson, Laurence G., *The Chinese Way in Religion.* Encino, Calif. and Belmont, Calif.: Dickenson Publishing Co., Inc., 1973. See Part Five: Family Religion.

Freedman, Maurice, "Ancestor Worship: Two Facets of the Chinese Case," in Maurice Freedman, ed., *Social Organization. Essays Presented to Raymond Firth.* Chicago, Aldine Publishers, 1967. Study by an eminent anthropologist.

Wolf, Arthur P., "Chinese Kinship and Mourning Dress," in Maurice Freedman, ed., *Family and Kinship in Chinese Society.* Stanford, Calif., Stanford University Press, 1970, pp. 189–207. Reveals how new ways of analyzing familiar data can shed unexpected light on both Chinese kinship and religion.

Ahern, Emily M., *The Cult of the Dead in a Chinese Village.* Stanford, Calif., Stanford University Press, 1973. Another demonstration of the valuable new insights being afforded through application of anthropological theory. Admirably lucid style.

*It is hardly necessary to point out that, while genealogies may contain a considerable element of fiction, this is immaterial so far as their validity and function for the family and lineage members are concerned.

4.
The Community: Gods and Temples

Religious Needs Beyond the Kinship Group

The ancestral cult is basic to Chinese religion because it is the one universal institution and because it molded Chinese society into its traditional form. And yet despite this form, in which the interests, responsibilities, and loyalties tended to be focused inward to the family and lineage rather than outward to the public realm, there did exist, in fact, important extra-kinship social groups, such as the local community, the nation, and the occupational guilds. The family therefore did not claim the individual one hundred per cent. Furthermore, in China as elsewhere, there were many individuals whose needs drove them to seek satisfaction outside of the kinship and secular institutions. Such persons would join a private religious club, become lay devotees of Buddhism or Taoism, or actually take the tonsure and become monks or nuns. The religious expressions of the individual will be discussed in Chapter 6; here we shall consider the religious life of the community as it has been manifested in the popular cults.

The folk religion with its deities, as described below, dates from around the end of the Han dynasty, about A.D. 200. The character of folk religion in earlier ages is obscure. But in general, the difference between the two stages is the admixture of Buddhism and "religious Taoism" that began in the latter half of the Han period.

The Gods

General Characteristics. Regardless of the origin or significance of the deities, they are nearly all humanized by the popular religion. That is to say, they have acquired biographies that tell of their human lives—lives marked by omens, precocious superhuman powers and signs, of course. Thus, they are not merely anthropomorphic, but they were actually human in their earlier term, just like the ancestor-gods. This is not to say that all deities were historical persons. Many were originally merely personifications of natural phenomena such as wind, rain, rivers, mountains, and stars, while many were legendary figures. Still others have been fabricated out of whole cloth and may be called fictitious, such as certain characters in a novel of the Ming dynasty (1368–1644) called *The Canonization of the Gods.* Some are survivals of antique nature worship, some are Taoist masters who attained immortality and the ability to work big magic, some are

Indian Buddhist importations or Chinese Buddhist creations, some are famous statesmen or generals or just and merciful magistrates, some are men or women of the people who manifested strange, miraculous powers. There are deities whose popularity has endured for centuries all over the country, and there are many more that gained only local fame, passing into oblivion after a short time. In the lively phrase of Maspero, "it is an unheard-of swarm of gods and spirits of every kind, an innumerable rabble."[1]

The Western observer, accustomed to require a serious theological explanation for deity, finds in this casual, unsystematic pantheon an intolerably profane character. The Western mind, long under the conviction that there is only one God, and that polytheism is utter blasphemy, resists the possibility that belief in the existence of "an innumerable rabble" of gods and spirits can be equated with true religion. The God of Western religion is unimaginably superior to man, omnipotent, the Source and Creator of all being, love incarnate, and so forth; whereas these gods of the Chinese popular religion are hardly more than human beings deified, possessed of mysterious and supernatural powers, of course, and yet far closer to man than to God. The Western believer may beseech God to grant personal favors, and yet he likes to think that he approaches God fundamentally in a spirit of pure, disinterested worship; while the Chinese attitude before their deities seems in contrast so selfish, so devoid of the rapture of adoration. One is tempted to put it into an aphorism: Western man worships God as almighty because God made him; the Chinese demand service from their gods because man made them.

The gods are alive because they have manifested themselves through their works. Their spiritual power, called *ling* in Chinese, is the evidence of their existence. This is why, to borrow another apt remark from Maspero, "people become gods every day in China."[2] Any claim or attribution of *ling* that gains a certain public currency may result in deification of a person. Rumors having spread and credibility having been established through confirmation that the spirit responds to prayers, a temple will be put up through public subscription. From then on the growth or decline of the cult is a matter of god's efficacy. This means that the death of the gods is also commonplace. When public confidence in the power of a deity has waned, he will be neglected and eventually forgotten.

This continuing process of obsolescence is responsible for the fact that while there are innumerable gods whose names and biographies may be found in the extensive hagiological literature of Taoism and Buddhism and on the rolls of the State religion, in the actual religious life of the people at any one time or place there is a fairly limited number of them. The interest of the local community in their gods is a matter of their usefulness, and hardly extends to historical information about them—except, of course, insofar as that information as popularly known fixes their particular area of spiritual power, their specific sort of *ling*.

It is this specialization in power, rather than origins or titles, which sets the deities off as individuals. They are not personifications of abstract virtues or passions or activities like Greek gods, but rather more like human officials who

Top, Taoist priest with magical sword and symbolical pennant. *Middle,* House-sized altar, constructed of paper and bamboo and decorated with colorful folk art, erected in a field in Taiwan for important religious festival. *Bottom,* carrying an image of Lao Tzu, supposed founder of Taoism, in a palanquin in a parade.

have the power to grant or withhold favors within the limits of their own jurisdiction. Many of them are indeed designated as officials in the spiritual hierarchy, counterparts to the bureaucrats in the old Imperial tables of organization. Such deities may be known as individuals by name, but more often they are simply known by the titles of their offices. The vast spiritual bureaucracy is well organized on paper, but again the people know little and care less about the systematic formalizations in the books.

A Sampler of the Gods from Taiwan Province. To illustrate some of the generalities expressed thus far we shall in this section describe the major deities of the folk religion in present-day Taiwan.[3] According to a religious census published in 1960, there were in Taiwan, for a population of about ten million, well over four thousand temples of all sorts. Enthroned as chief deities in these temples were eighty-six different gods. Although this seems to be a large pantheon, a relatively small number of deities commanded by far the greatest share of popularity. There were nine with over one hundred temples each; these we may call the major deities. Another nineteen had at least twenty temples apiece. The other fifty-eight gods in Taiwan are of only minor importance to the folk religion.

The deities are not necessarily individuals. They also include groups and "multiples." An example of a group would be the "Kings of the Three-Mountains Country" (see below). By "multiples" is meant deities identified by title or office rather than as individuals. The local earth gods would be examples of this type. Of the nine major deities, six are individuals, two are multiple, and there is one group.

1. *Wang-yeh.* "Kings." Tutelary gods of immigrants from Fukien province, across the Taiwan Strait, whose descendants comprise four- fifths of the local population (by "local population" we mean to except those "mainlanders" who fled to Taiwan when the mainland fell to the Communists after World War II). These gods illustrate the vagueness about biographical facts mentioned above: one opinion is that they are the souls of loyal ministers of the Han and T'ang dynasties; but another opinion holds that they are the souls of 360 scholar-officials of the late Ming dynasty. Several may be enshrined in a single temple. They are said to ward off pestilence and to aid storm-tossed mariners.

2. *Kuan-yin Fo-tsu.* No doubt the most popular deity in all of China; every foreign account of Chinese culture mentions this so-called Goddess of Mercy. Originally *Kuan-yin* was a bodhisattva called in Indian Buddhist texts Avalokiteśvara, one of the two assistants of the Buddha Amitābha. The Buddhist origin is indicated in the title *Fo-tsu,* meaning literally "Buddha-ancestor" and also used to indicate the Patriarchs of Buddhist sects. Although still one of the major figures found in purely Buddhist temples, *Kuan-yin* was long ago taken to the hearts of the masses and transformed into a compassionate mother figure. In the folk religion she is the embodiment of loving kindness, giver of male children to childless wives, and source of help in time of need.

3. *T'ien-shang Sheng-mu.* "Holy Mother in Heaven." Despite this title, she is in no way similar to the Holy Mary of Catholicism. She provides a classic example of the process by which "people become gods every day in China." The beginnings of the cult are obscure, but the generally accepted story is that she was born in the year the Sung dynasty was founded (A.D. 960) on the island of Meichou just off the coast of Fukien province. Her birth was attended by auspicious portents. She was an exceptionally pious girl, and at the age of thirteen she met a Taoist master who presented her with certain charms and other secret lore. When she was sixteen she manifested her magical power by saving the lives of her father and elder brother, whose boat had capsized. Other tales of her supernatural intervention were told by grateful recipients of her mercies. When she died, still a young girl, a temple was erected in her community, seeking to attract her continuing favors.

As decades and then centuries passed, stories of miracles wrought by the goddess accumulated all up and down the southeastern seaboard, and she became a familiar guardian spirit, particularly among seafarers. By mid-twelfth century the Imperial Court itself had learned of her reputation for spiritual power, and gave her official recognition as a deity of national importance. This meant that the State incorporated her worship in the schedule of sacrifices to be performed by the bureaucracy throughout the land.

The cult continued to grow until the goddess became one of the major deities of southeastern China and the most important deity of sailors, fishermen, and all who must hazard their lives upon the waters. She received high titles by imperial decree; for example, in 1409: *t'ien fei,* "Imperial Concubine of Heaven," who "protects the country and shelters the people, looks after [those who call on her] with mysterious *ling,* and saves universally by her great kindness." This imposing title was elevated by the K'ang Hsi Emperor in 1683 to *t'ien hou,* "Consort of Heaven." To the people, she is more familiarly known as *Ma-tsu,* a Fukienese word for grandma.

4. *Fu-teh Cheng-shen.* "True god of blessings and virtue." The local earth god (*t'u-ti*) found everywhere in China, this "multiple" deity is most numerous because every tiny residential area, even every home, has its own god. Because of his prominence in the Chinese religion, every work on the subject has discussed the *t'u-ti.* His temples are commonly small and unimpressive, he may even have to make do without a shrine. But the humbleness of his shrines is rather an indication of his closeness to the people than of any contempt for him. It is the earth god who is, in fact, most intimately involved in their lives:

> . . . They are the gods of their district, so they protect, care for, and control the locality. The people have come to appeal to them for everything which effects their lives. All births and deaths are reported to them. In cases of danger to the community, they are taken from their little temple, and placed where they may see all that is happening. In this way they are thought to better understand the conditions, and be more ready in their assistance. They are thought especially to protect their worshippers against mildew, locusts, and caterpillars, or to permit the crops of the one

neglecting them to be destroyed. As the people believe a faithful heart will gain their favor, and bring a rich harvest, they are continually found in worship before their shrines. . . .

In addition to the Earth Gods of the locality, there are the little T'u Ti of the home. These little images are found in nearly every household. They usually are kept on the floor under the altar board; thus they are as close to the Earth as possible. They are supposed to control the particular spot on which the building rests, and thus be a protection to the house and its inmates. . . .[4]

5. *Shih-chia* Fo. Śakyamuni Buddha. Although he occupies a position of central importance in purely Buddhist establishments, he has not usually been so popular in the community religion. His current prominence in Taiwan is a phenomenon of post-World War II years.

6. *Hsüan t'ien Shang ti.* "Emperor-on-High of the Dark Quarter." Also commonly known as *Pei-chi Yu-sheng Chen-chün,* "Protecting Holy True Lord of the North Pole [Star]," he is the sole survivor in the living religion of the spirits who in high antiquity ruled the four quarters of the universe. In more recent centuries his function has become generalized as a protector, as in the case of many warrior-type figures in the popular pantheon, and this function is reflected in the title by which he is best known as a national deity throughout China: *Chen-wu Ta-ti,* "Truly Military Great Emperor."

He is reported in the official histories to have appeared to Emperor Hui Tsung (reigned 1101–1126) of the Sung dynasty, an accomplished painter, and the likeness sketched by the emperor is the prototype of his modern image:

> Usually an armed squire is placed behind him, carrying his black banner; the god himself is set on the back of the tortoise encircled by the serpent, and floating on the waters, as is fitting, since he is the ruler of the North, and water is the element corresponding to the northern quarter.
>
> This tortoise and this serpent upon which he rests are interpreted in totally different ways by the various Chinese authors: to some they are two celestial officers placed under his orders; according to others, they are, on the contrary, enemy demons whom he has conquered, and whom he is treading under his feet. In point of fact, the wreathed serpent and tortoise are the god himself in his first shape, more ancient than the present anthropomorphic personage. They are met with from the time of the Han dynasty as the symbol of the Northern region of the world in the funeral chambers of the second century, where they face the Red Bird, the symbol of the South, and are opposed to the White Tiger (the West) and the Green Dragon (the East).[5]

7. *Kuan Sheng-ti-chün.* "Holy Emperor-Lord Kuan." The warrior-protector *par excellence;* Western authors generally call him *Kuan Ti,* "Emperor Kuan." He will serve as a good example of the historical personage deified. In the romantically pictured epoch of the Three Kingdoms (A.D. 220–265), Kuan Yü (to use his mortal name) was one of a famous trio of generals. His character and exploits were popularized in the great work of historical fiction entitled *The Romance of the Three Kingdoms,* written during the fourteenth century. The extraordinary success of this novel was not confined to those sufficiently literate to read it, but was spread among the entire populace through the medium of the

storytellers and the stage. It is quite accurate to say that it not only supplanted the official records of the period in the Chinese mind, but gave every rustic an astonishing familiarity with the pseudo-history of Kuan Yü and his companions and foes. Through the centuries his cult as a martial hero, protecting against evil spirits, has become ever more popular. In addition to his basic protective function, he is also a patron saint of literature and of commerce.

8. *Pao-sheng Ta-ti.* "Great Emperor Who Preserves Life." Here is a deity who, while of major importance in Taiwan, does not seem to be known nationally. He is a specialist in healing the sick, a role that is also played by several other gods. In his mortal life he was a doctor of Ch'üanchou prefecture in Fukien province, and his devotees in Taiwan are descendants of Ch'üanchou immigrants. His mortal name was Wu Pen, which accounts for another appellation by which he is commonly known, *Wu Chen-jen,* "Wu, the True Man"—*chen-jen* being a technical term in Taoism for those who have perfected themselves in the arts of immortality. He is said to have cured an empress of the Sung dynasty, as well as a tiger whose throat was obstructed by the bones of a woman he had eaten. The grateful tiger became a guardian spirit in Wu Pen's temples after the latter had been deified. It will again illustrate the indifference to historical fact to mention that *Pao-sheng Ta-ti* is also said by some Taiwanese to be the soul of an entirely different man, likewise a physician, but alive during the T'ang dynasty, half a millennium earlier than the time of Wu Pen.

9. *San-shan-kuo Wang.* "Kings of the Three-Mountains Country." The country to which the title refers is the homeland of Hakka immigrants, in Kuang-tung province. The Hakka are a distinctive minority group of Chinese who make up about one-fifth of the local Taiwanese population. These tutelary deities were brought by their forefathers during the seventeenth and eighteenth centuries. The kings are a group of spirits of three mountains which are said to have assisted the imperial troops in putting down an insurrection in the region during the T'ang dynasty. In gratitude for their help they were canonized by imperial decree. This may serve as a good example of animism in the folk religion extended further into the religion of the State.

Temples and Their Functioning

The deities are housed in temples that may be called palaces. That is to say, they are the official residences of their exalted inhabitants, rather than gathering places for a congregation. Temples vary from unpretentious to grand, from one-room structures no bigger than a dog kennel to complexes of halls arranged row on row and separated by spacious courtyards. Despite a thousand variations, they share a similarity in appearance because all Chinese buildings, sacred or secular, derive from the same architectural principles. The temple is therefore just a more or less elaborately ornamented version of the Chinese "basic building":

1. It is in a compound surrounded by a wall.
2. The main entrance is in the south face of the wall. Since hoary antiquity all Chinese buildings wherever possible have been oriented along a north-south axis; the

master—emperor, household head, or god—sits in the north facing south. The entranceway is a triple gate of which each doorway is closed by heavy double wooden leaves. The whole of this entranceway is recessed within the wall and covered by a truncated version of a building roof. It is raised above ground level, and one enters by ascending several stone steps. The doors are painted with the guardian figures of warrior-generals who stand in protective stances to keep out evil spirits.

3. Stepping through the gate one finds oneself in the gatehouse. From here one looks into a square of buildings with a courtyard in the middle. The buildings running longitudinally on the east and west are subsidiary, used for the daily living purposes of the temple's caretakers, or perhaps housing subordinate deities in the side chapels. The main hall (or halls, if there are several) runs transversely, and is commonly divided into a large room in the center flanked by side rooms on east and west. The center room may be distinguished by a double roof, and its entranceway is similar to the main gate.

4. All of the buildings are raised off the ground on platforms of pounded earth faced with stone, and are entered by ascending stone steps.

5. The buildings are essentially wooden frames, whose most important features are the rows of sturdy round pillars defining the size and outline of the structure, and the unique system of beams and brackets which supports the roof. The walls, whether external or internal, play no structural role, but are in effect screens. The outside walls are commonly brick, the inside walls may be brick or wood, and may or may not reach the ceiling (since there may or may not be a ceiling).

6. The most striking part of the temple is the roof, that unmistakably "Chinese" feature. Instead of simply sitting on the walls like the typical Western roof, it looks to be, as it structurally is, independent of the building itself; and therefore one has the impression that it is light and free despite its relatively massive proportions. The eaves extend well out beyond the walls, forming a sort of canopy over the building. In northern China the curve of the eaves is moderate and the ends are short, giving a rather sober effect. On southern temples, however, the eaves soar outward and upward in great arcs, with long-stretching tips. Along the ridge and the eaves are ornamental pottery figures of mythical birds and beasts, and legendary humans. Again, these are more numerous and exuberant in execution in the southern style. Finally, whenever financial resources permit the roof will be covered with special colored tiles.

7. The colorfulness of the roof is matched by the walls, posts, and interior decoration of the building. The Chinese preference is for strong colors—red, blue, green, gold, white, black. The posts are bright Chinese red, and the doors likewise. Down the pillars and across horizontal plaques here and there are pious mottoes and quotations from the sacred books inscribed in gold. The ceiling, if there is one, is also for ornamental purposes, serving as a gorgeously painted canopy over all or part of the room. Otherwise the complex structure of the rugged beams with their specifically Chinese bracketing system is left exposed.

8. If the compound contains more than one hall the first one will likely be used to house lesser deities, while the principal deity will be enthroned in a rear hall. His dignities are again a matter of the financial resources available. At the very least the icon will be the size of a doll, seated on a table, with the altar before him bearing the customary sacrificial utensils. At the other extreme the deity will be represented by an image life-size or larger, not only painted and gilded, but garbed in beautifully embroidered robes and fitted with a glittering crown. He sits on a throne within an

Top left, typical temple in Taiwan. *Top right*, fortune-teller's office in a temple. *Bottom left*, warriors who guard temple gates. *Bottom right*, believers and their offerings.

臺灣省天后宮

第九號

乙巳　屬火利在夏天宜其南方　解曰

龍虎相隨在深山
君爾何須背後看
不知此去相愛悷
他日與我却無干

（龍虎相會）

六甲先男高貴
作事難成
婚姻不可
大命險寅辰日過不畏
月令不遂破錢有口舌
官事難光局破錢
耕作晚好
種珠不可

出外不可
求財無
失物難尋
功名無
移居不可
買男兒不可

臺北市成都路四九號之一

Left, charm from a Taiwanese temple. The symbol of the *t'ai-chi*, or cosmic unity, surrounded by the eight trigrams, lends power to the charm for protection, good luck, and family peace. *Right*, oracle from a temple of T'ien-hou, Imperial Consort of Heaven (Matsu).

elaborately carved wooden shrine, covered by a resplendent baldachin. On his left (the place of honor in China) and right hands will stand smaller figures as his attendants. If he is a god of high rank, these attendants may themselves be important deities.

9. If the temple is of any size there will be deities other than the principal god enthroned there. These may be ranged along the sides of the main hall, or may be housed in separate chapels. In the popular religion a temple is apt to have quite a mixed company of the gods, including those from the Buddhist and Taoist pantheons as well as the particular deities favored by the local community.

The smallest temples, as we have mentioned, are no more than tiny shrines. Such temples, housing the local earth god or other spirits that may be humble in rank but very close to the daily lives of the people, are found everywhere, in the busy streets of a town and out in the fields of the countryside. Their occupants must often be contented with a plain brick altar and no ornamentation whatever; in fact the deity himself may be represented by no more than a tablet or even just a rude inscription.

Temples are so conspicuous everywhere in China that one is at a loss to account for the claim of so many foreign writers that the Chinese are an irreligious people. Even aside from the ubiquitous small shrines just described, every village and every small subsection of a town or city will have its community temples, generally the largest and most ostentatious structures in the neighborhood. Such a temple functions not only as a religious center for the community, but often as a schoolroom, meeting place for community business, playground for youngsters, and threshing floor at harvest time. The construction of temples was a major expense to the local people, and the fact that the people would give so much of their meager income is in itself impressive proof of their sincere belief in the efficacy of the deities.

Community temples would be under the overall management of a local committee, and might or might not have the permanent services of a resident priest or medium. The priests and mediums might belong to the Taoist order whose vocation was noncelibate and whose function was the practice of magic and exorcism. They thus served as religious "technicians," and were in no sense spiritual leaders of the community.

The doors of the temple would stand open at all times. Individuals may come at any time to bring their personal problems to the god. One lights several sticks of incense and places them in the brazier on the altar, bows or prostrates oneself before the altar, perhaps burns mock paper money, or offers sacrificial edibles. The god is asked for help on a wide variety of matters (see Chapter 2). Very often he is consulted as to the advisability of taking some course of action. This is done by several divinatory techniques, of which a common one is to throw on the floor two pieces of wood shaped like the halves of a fat banana that has been sliced lengthwise. The positive or negative response of the god is indicated by the manner in which the pieces land on their flat or rounded sides. The altar is provided with a vase containing many long, narrow bamboo slips, each numbered. The supplicant shakes the vase until one slip protrudes above the rest. Taking this slip to the attendant, the latter gives the inquirer a printed oracle from the set numbered in accordance with the bamboo slips. In many temples there is also a fortune teller who is frequently consulted for the reading of horoscopes and who serves as amanuensis for the illiterate.

Besides these commonplace, everyday functions, there are certain times when the temple is thronged with people and abustle with activity. One biographical fact about the god will be known to all—his birthday. This is the festival of the god, marked by ceremonies, processions, feasting, and theatricals. We quote from the eyewitness account of an experienced observer:

On August 2, 1930, at the town of Li t'o, west of Yuchow [in Szechwan province], the writer witnessed a *I'u-tsu-hui*, or a festival on the birthday of the god of earth, or the Lord of Earth. There was a procession along the city streets, which were literally packed with sightseers and worshipers. Along the way there were many offerings of pork and beans, and much lighting of candles and incense and burning of spirit money. Many who participated in the parade had their faces painted with odd streaks of gold, and black and white paint, and wore caps on which mottoes were written. People of both sexes and of all ages marched in the parade, some of them carrying small sticks of decorated wood. It is believed that the festival causes the crops to prosper, heals diseases, and wards off calamities.

In the parade were two pavilions in which were hats, shoes, candles, and many dresses and gowns. Then came a large, red-faced god, with a fan in his hand, carried in a pavilion or large sedan chair on the shoulders of coolies. Three bombs, or short guns, were occasionally set off to announce the coming of the god, and a band played typical Chinese music. Following the god were scores of common people, each carrying a wooden placard. As the god passed by, he was loudly hailed by the spectators, some of whom carried in their arms infants whom they wished the god to bless and protect. Following those who carried the placards were musicians with gongs, timbrels, and horns. Next came Ch'uan Chu, the Lord of Szechwan, who was dressed in yellow silk embroidered garments. In the center of his forehead he had a third eye which enabled him to see good and evil, and such invisible creatures as demons. As Ch'uan Chu passed along, people bowed their heads to the ground in reverent worship. After the god came a squad of soldiers to preserve order.

In the parade were people who were strikingly dressed; some had their faces painted. They participated in the procession in performance of vows. When they were sick, or were faced with some dreadful calamity, they prayed to the god for relief, and promised that if they were helped they would participate in this way in the procession on the birthday of the god. The number of people who thus took part in the procession each year seems to the common people to prove the efficacy of the god.

A witness of this procession could see clearly that the people were emotionally thrilled and deeply impressed; that emotions of reverence, awe, and wonder were aroused; and that unconsciously the people received a vivid impression of the greatness of the gods, and were made more loyal to them, the priests, and the religion. The techniques used are admirable for making such impressions on the minds of the simple people, and are evidently the result of centuries of experience.[6]

It is interesting to note that the Chinese case is no exception to the general rule that theatricals are originally closely connected with religion. Although the contents of the plays that have been popular on the boards in China for the past several centuries are not in themselves religious, the performances are thought to entertain the gods as well as their human audiences. Therefore, no festival should be without its theatricals, and in a temple of any pretensions there will be a place for these, even if it is only a small courtyard.

Since the Chinese drama requires very little in the way of properties there is no difficulty in the arrangements. A makeshift stage is quickly erected, cloth backdrops are suspended on bamboo poles. The audience clusters at the front and sides, standing to watch and listen, coming or going at will. A band of perhaps a half-dozen instruments, with percussion predominating, supports the singers and directs their highly stylized movements. The stories are all well known to the most rustic audience, consisting of traditional plots from history and fiction, and they always emphasize the triumph of the conventional morality. The principal actors are appreciated for their skill in the prescribed pantomiming, for their acrobatic feats in the case of plays of military action, and above all for their singing—the drama being something of a blend of ballet and opera. Naturally the troupes that play the countryside and perform for the temple festivals are but crude facsimiles of the artists popular in the great cities of culture; but then, their rural audiences (and the gods themselves) probably enjoy them at least as much as the pampered critics enjoy the most refined productions.

SELECTED READINGS

Yang, C. K., *Religion in Chinese Society.* Berkeley and Los Angeles: University of Califor-nia Press, 1961; papercover available. Best exposition of the subject.

Bodde, Derk, "Myths of Ancient China," in S. N. Kramer (ed.) *Mythologies of the Ancient World.* New York: Anchor Books, 1961 (papercover). Brief but authoritative.

Maspero, Henri, "The Mythology of Modern China," in J. Hackin *et al., Asiatic Mythol-ogy.* New York: Thomas Y. Crowell Co., n.d.; reprinted 1963. The author is a leading authority. His treatment of the subject is interesting although somewhat unsys-tematic.

Day, Clarence B., *Chinese Peasant Cults, Being a Study of Chinese Paper Gods.* Shanghai: Kelly & Walsh, Ltd., 1940. Reprinted in Taipei by Ch'eng Wen Publishing Co., 1969. Thorough study by a missionary scholar; well illustrated.

Goodrich, Anne Swann, *The Peking Temple of the Eastern Peak.* Nagoya (Japan): Monu-menta Serica, 1964. Detailed study of the pantheon as found in one of Peking's most famous temples; copiously illustrated.

Hodous, Lewis, *Folkways in China.* London: Arthur Probsthain, 1929. Some major deities, and the round of the festival year, especially in Foochow area.

Burkhardt, V. R., *Chinese Creeds and Customs.* Hong Kong: South China Morning Post, Ltd. 1953–58, 3 vols. A melange of brief articles about folk religion and community festivals in the Hong Kong area.

Thompson, Laurence G., *The Chinese Way in Religion.* Encino, Calif., and Belmont, Calif.: Dickenson Publishing Co., Inc. 1973. See Part Six: Popular Religion.

5.

The State: Emperor and Officials

State Religion and Confucianism

From the functional point of view the religion of the Chinese State may be seen to have fulfilled two purposes. One was the religious purpose *per se,* deriving from the belief that the emperor, and by extension his official servants, had an essential part to play in mediating between the forces of nature and the lives of the people; the other was the political and social purpose, in which temples and rituals and the conferring of official titles upon important national deities were means, consciously utilized, to fortify the position of the ruling dynasty and strengthen the prestige of the government. It would be naïve to overlook the latter purpose, but it is being overly cynical to deny the former.

The state religion has often been equated with "Confucianism." However, its essential features long antedate the adoption of Confucian teachings as the official orthodoxy during the Former Han Dynasty[1]—or even Confucius himself (551–479 B.C.). The sacrificial rituals, and the sorts of deities to which the sacrifices were offered, can be traced back as far as archeological evidence is found, into the Shang dynasty. These deities were either the more conspicuous phenomena of nature or else the ancestors, as we have seen in Chapter 4. A third category of official deification seems to have come into the official liturgy during Former Han times: the public worship of the souls of great men. Although Confucius himself was the "great man" *par excellence,* he obviously would not have approved of this sort of worship. We have earlier quoted his dictum that "sacrifices to spirits which are not those of one's own dead is [mere] flattery."

What is meant by the statement that Confucianism was adopted as the state orthodoxy? To put it as simply as possible, it means that the ancient writings identified with the Confucian school were exalted above all others, that the basis of all formal education was this Confucian Bible, that entrance into the privileged class of scholar-bureaucrats was almost limited to those having some mastery of this literature, and that ultimately all these conditions molded the Chinese state and much of Chinese culture. So far as religion was concerned, it means that the whole weight of the rationalistic, humanistic character of Confucian thought was thrown against the development of institutionalized religions such as Taoism or Buddhism. Certainly the state could not do without religion, but the religious ideas and forms were those inherited from antiquity as preserved in the Confucian Canon.

It was a religion in which the emperor personally officiated at the supreme sacrifices, and his Confucian bureaucrats officiated at the lower level throughout the land; thus, there was no separate estate of priests. Insofar as the scholars who codified the worship and rituals were of the Confucian school, and insofar as the operation of the state cults was a part of the duties of all officials, the religion of the state can of course be described as Confucian. But like their Master, the Confucian literati thought of themselves as "transmitters rather than creators," and their writings on sacrifices and rituals were but refinements of the doctrines inherited from high antiquity.

One component of the state religion was the cult of the Confucius himself, who was naturally regarded by the literati as their patron saint. Every craft and occupation in China had its patron deity, and Confucius might therefore be considered as just another of these—except that the craft of the scholars was governing the people and their occupation was official service. The significance of the adoption of Confucianism as the state orthodoxy was thus that the rulers of China recognized the unique usefulness to government of the Confucian theories and training. Or at least, if they actually found other methods more useful in many cases, it was expedient for them to give lip service to the high ideals of Confucian teachings. Consequently, they saw the desirability of exalting the Master as a pillar of support for the imperial power. The sacrifices to Confucius were always, and appropriately, the responsibility of the literati-officials, but they were incorporated into the state cults and were even included in the limited group of sacrifices personally performed by the emperor, for what may be called political reasons.

As for the imperial sacrifices, they were so important, and so colorful and dramatic, that they have sometimes been described as if they actually constituted the state religion of China. The sublime sacrifices performed by the emperor at the altars of Heaven and Earth particularly captured the attention of foreign writers in the nineteenth century, who furthermore, because most of them were missionaries, were most concerned with the question as to whether the object of this worship was the same as the true, Christian God. It is apparent that the imperial worship was indeed an important component of the state religion, but it was one component only. In this chapter we shall first discuss this imperial worship; next we shall consider the workings of the official religion in general terms; and finally we shall give particulars concerning the official religion as it operated at the local level.

Kingship and Imperial Worship

In ancient China as everywhere in the primitive world there would have been no meaningful distinction between the "political" and the "religious." The authority of chief or king could not exist without the sanction of religious qualifications claimed and acknowledged. An aura of divinity was indispensable to the charisma of a king. Such an inseparable association of ideas characterized not only primitive societies and the ancient world, but continued down to the recent past. The religious basis of kingship is proved, if such proof were necessary, by the rapid decline and virtual extinction of the institution once the "divine right" was no longer taken seriously.

We cannot doubt that the origin of kingship in China shared this character. We have already noted (see Chapter 3) that certain passages in the *Shu Ching (Canon of Historical Documents)* speak of the king's ancestors as dwelling with the Supreme Ruler in Heaven and as being able to influence the latter. We also mentioned the propagandistic intent manifest in a number of documents in this book, the purport of which was that the overthrow of the Shang and the establishment of the Chou kings constituted the will of the Supreme Ruler in Heaven. Much later, this concept of a "mandate of Heaven" was incorporated into orthodox Confucian political philosophy, its classical expression being given by Mencius (particularly in Book VA, chapters 5 and 6).

The peculiarity of this Chinese version of the divine right is that from the beginning, as found in *Shu Ching,* it was qualified in such a way as to preclude the divinity of the ruling house. To put it in a word, what Heaven gives, Heaven can also take away. No man could establish himself and his line on the Dragon Throne unless he had been accepted by Heaven as the True King; but no dynasty could continue to be acceptable to Heaven unless its kings *actually were* True Kings. There was no mystery about the reading of Heaven's will in the matter: this was manifested in the upshot of revolution. When unbearable conditions or vaulting ambition brought rebels up in arms against the government, if the government were able to put down the rebellion and execute its leaders, it was evident that the emperor still retained his mandate; but should one of the revolutionary leaders overthrow the government and set himself on the throne, it was on the contrary evident that Heaven had withdrawn its mandate from the former dynasty, and conferred it upon a new one.

In the Chinese system, therefore, divine right meant that the emperor held his office by virtue of a commission from Heaven, but it did not mean that the emperor was himself a divinity. It is remarkable that this theory of the mandate of Heaven retained its vitality throughout Chinese history in a polity which was an absolute despotism. The explanation is that the theory was embodied in the sacred literature of the Confucian literati, who in their capacity as bureaucrats were the indispensable mainstay of every emperor's administration. While it is going too far to characterize this theory as a "democratic force" in Chinese history, it was at least a factor of real significance in limiting the imperial will, for ultimately it was a justification of the right of revolution. Heaven was on the side of the righteous, whether that side represented the entrenched regime or the rebels.

In order to avoid loss of his mandate the ruler must benefit the people and give them a secure livelihood. Aside from the mundane policies required to carry out this responsibility, there were the moral and supernatural duties. As for morality, Confucian precept held that the people were the grass, and their betters the wind—that good or bad behavior of the people was a reflection of the moral example set by the ruler and his officials (see Chapter I). As for the supernatural, the ruler was held to be the leader and representative of Man, who formed a ternion with Heaven and Earth. This resulted from the gestalt cosmology that we discussed in our chapter on the world view: man was inseparably a part of nature, and therefore there was an interplay, a mutual reaction between the two. The function of the emperor was to play his proper part in maintaining the smooth coordination of this cooperative process, which meant insuring that men were properly and beneficially governed, and that they in turn did their (agricultural) work at the proper times and seasons and in the proper way.

The emperor's unique contribution to the coordination of man and nature, aside from supervising the administration of government, was to pay the appropriate ritual respects to the great powers of the universe. The latter was represented in the large by Heaven and Earth, which stood for the *yang* and *yin* forces and were spoken of in homely metaphor as male and female, husband and wife, emperor and empress of the universe. To these two great symbols of Nature the lord of all men sacrificed as the only Powers above his human power. To them he paid the utmost reverence, the threefold kneeling and ninefold prostration, and them alone he acknowledged as his own lord, in his prayer styling himself "your subject." To other impressive but obviously subsidiary powers of nature—the sun, the moon, and other heavenly bodies, the deities that controlled meteorological phenomena, the great mountains and rivers—he also sacrificed, but without humbling himself.

The emperor's humility before the altars of Heaven and Earth, far from lessening his prestige, was actually the ultimate sign of his legitimacy as ruler of men. Only the rightful ruler could perform this ritual, and its imitation by any other person was a declaration of rebellion. It is no wonder that it was made rich with a fascinating symbolism and designed to produce an overwhelmingly impressive effect.

Heaven and Earth were the emperor's symbolical parents, but he also had real, human parents. To them he owed the same obedience in life and worship after death that every Chinese son owed his parents. The imperial ancestors were naturally worshipped in more elaborate style than those of lesser persons, but the practices were essentially the same—dressing, coffining, entombing, setting up of the spirit tablet in the ancestral hall, and all. The *feng-shui* of their tombs was a matter of vital concern to the State because their occupants exercised influence over the reigning sovereign. These spirits dwelt in Heaven, where they presumably had the ear of the Supreme Ruler. This idea was clearly pictured in the arrangements at the altars of Heaven and Earth. At the top of the altar where the spirit tablet of Heaven or Earth was placed to receive the emperor's worship, the tablets of the imperial ancestors stood at the left and right hands, as if in attendance. This arrangement corresponds to that found in all temples, where the chief deity is flanked by subordinates. Or, if one prefers to think in terms of a Chinese feast—and *the sacrifice is essentially a feast for the divinity* (not an act of atonement)—it is like the guest of honor flanked by what the Chinese call *p'ei-k'o* or accompanying guests. But in fact it is a representation of the ancient theory we cited from *Shu Ching* (see Chapter 3, pp. 43 f), and the spirit tablet of Heaven still, in the nineteenth century, bore the ancient name: it read in full, *Huang T'ien Shang Ti,* which may be understood either as Shang Ti [in] August Heaven, or as August Heaven:: Shang Ti.

The Official Religion

We said above that the principal objects of the state worship were very ancient, long antedating even Confucius. According to archeological evidence, in the late Shang or Yin age (roughly 1300–1100 B.C.), the following deities were worshipped in addition to the all-important ancestors:

> First of all, there was the Supreme God, the highest of all deities, that was called *Ti.* The position of *Ti* in heaven was somewhat like that of the king on earth. *Ti* was also called *Shang Ti.* . . .
>
> There were also God of wind, called "Ti's Messenger," and God of Cloud, called "Six Clouds"—meaning the clouds in the East, West, South, North, above the earth and below the earth. The God of Sun was worshipped at sunrise and sunset. There was a God of Moon; and the lunar eclipse was considered as a portent of evil. Some of the conspicuous stars and constellations were also worshipped, for instance, Aldebaran or alpha of the Hyades.
>
> In many of the oracles, the worship of Yüeh and Ho was mentioned. Though the two characters have been interpreted as names of ancestors, yet the reading of the contexts convinces us that we should take them at their literal meaning: i.e., *Yüeh* means the mountain and *Ho* means the yellow River. There were gods for the four directions of the compass, as the worship of them is mentioned in the oralces [*sic*]. Gods of different localities and gods of certain big rivers, for instance, the Hwan, near the capital were constant objects of worship.[2]

For comparison, here are the deities named in the Ch'ing government regulations of the seventeenth century as recipients of official worship:

> Following the ancient classification the beings worshipped were arranged in three ranks.
>
> In the first rank were placed *Huang T'ien Shang Ti.* . . . The Empress Earth, the Imperial Ancestors and the Guardian Spirits of the Land and the Harvests [*she chi*]. To these in the year 1907 there was added the great Sage Confucius, who had previously been placed in the second rank.
>
> Others of the second rank were the Sun, the Moon, the Emperors and Kings of preceeding dynasties, the patron saint of Agriculture, the patroness of Sericulture, the Spirits of Heaven, the Spirits of Earth, and the Year Star, that is to say, the planet Jupiter, by whose revolution around the sun the Chinese calendar was regulated.
>
> In the third rank of this pantheon were the patron saint of Medicine, the God of War, the God of Literature, the North Star, the Eastern Peak, the tutelary deity of Peking, the God of Fire, the Dragon of the Black Dragon Pool (near Peking), the dragon of the Jade Fountain (near Peking) and that of the *K'un Ming* Lake (at the Summer Palace), the God of Artillery, the *Hou T'u* or God of the Soil, the *Ssu Kung*

or patron of the Mechanic arts, the God of the Furnace, the God of the Granary, the door gods and a number of canonized patriots, whose company has increased from generation to generation.[3]

All these deities receiving official worship of the first two ranks in modern times were worshipped during the Shang, or at the latest during early Chou times, with the exception, of course, of Confucius. The third rank includes mostly deities who became popular after the Han dynasty (ended A.D. 221) and those (such as the dragons) who are especially connected with Peking as the capital during the reign of the Manchu dynasty.

The calendar of official sacrifices was determined by the Board of Astronomy according to divinatory procedures and was published well in advance by the Ministry of Rites (*Li Pu*). This ministry was from the most remote times one of the major organs of government. Traditional accounts take it back to the as-yet legendary Hsia dynasty, which is supposed to have preceded Shang in the eighteenth century B.C. The feudal courts in Chou China would, of course, have required the services of specialists in sacrifices and protocol. With the formation of the imperial polity in Ch'in and Han times the Ministry of Rites essentially assumed the form it was to retain until the end of the empire. Its head was one of the nine great ministers of the administrative departments. Under him came various subdepartments and bureaus, most important of which was the Imperial Academy. "In so far as he supervised the Imperial Academy the Minister of Ceremonies performed the same duties as a Minister of Education in the present Chinese Government." But he could also be "described as a chief priest in the government," because he "is said to have been 'in charge of the ceremonies in the Imperial ancestral temples' and 'in charge of the worship of Heaven and Earth.' "[4]

During the latest (Ch'ing) dynasty, the Ministry of Rites performed the same sorts of functions as in Han times. Its educational responsibilities were still most important, but one of its five bureaus was the Bureau of Sacrificial Rites, "for state sacrifices and funerals, conferring of posthumous favors, editing the calendar, and miscellaneous sacrifices. . . . [The Ministry] kept records of all ceremonies the emperor attended, records of the descendants of Confucius, of Buddhist, Taoist, medical and astronomical officials in addition to those connected with education. It is [*sic*] reported to the emperor for rewards all cases of filial piety, righteousness, or loyalty."[5]

The performance of the official worship was regulated by detailed instructions circulated to all government offices (*yamen*) throughout the empire:

> Worship of the various gods and saints of the pantheon consisted in bathing, fasting, prostrations, prayers, and thanksgiving offerings of incense, lighted candles, gems, fruits, cooked food, salted vegetables and shew bread, libations of wine, sacrifices of whole oxen, sheep and pigs, sometimes deer and other game and, on certain occasions, a burnt sacrifice of a whole bullock, accompanied by music, and posturing or dancing.
>
> All sacrifices to deities of the first rank had to be preceded by three days of fasting, those to deities of the second rank by two days of fasting . . . Fasting did not mean

entire abstinence from all food, but from *hun,* i.e., from flesh and strong-smelling vegetables, such as leeks, garlic and onions; also from wine and all strong drink. No criminal proceedings were to be held; no invitations to feasts issued or accepted. There was to be no music. No inquiries after the sick were allowed and there must be no mourning for the dead. One was especially forbidden to enter the death chamber of a woman, to sacrifice to spirits and to sweep the tombs. All association of any kind with the sick and the mourner was prohibited. . . .

Special officers were appointed also to visit and inspect the various yamens, and any officer found neglecting the fast was punished according to law. . . .

The object of the bathing and fasting was to make oneself pure in body and heart and worthy to approach into the divine presence.[6]

Aside from those personified forces of nature whose worship had come down from archaic times, and aside from the imperial ancestral spirits, the deities on the official registers had achieved their position by a process with which our previous discussion of the folk religion has made us familiar. The efficacy of a spirit, manifested by deeds, would bring it fame over a widening area until it impressed the officials as being important enough to recommend it to the Throne. Eventually the emperor would confer a rank and title upon the spirit, exactly as upon a meritorious human subject. The government's patronage would extend further to bearing the cost of founding or renovating temples to the deity. In this way what had been only a local cult would become a part of the official religion. The process clearly exemplified the dual religious and political purpose of that religion: certainly the State was anxious to have whatever supernatural assistance might be available, while at the same time, by its patronage of the deities, it tacitly asserted its control over them. In other words, the fact that the emperor could confer ranks and titles and assign posts to the spiritual beings was clearcut evidence that his authority extended over the spiritual dimension as well as the world of men.

Official Religion at the Local Level*

Strictly speaking, there were no "local" officials in the Chinese empire. That is to say, all officials were members of the imperial government, appointed usually after passing competitive civil service examinations and then posted, shifted about, and given assignments at the discretion of the personnel department at the Capital. To guard against the interference of family connections with an official's duties, it was the practice not to assign him to his home region, so that every official was a stranger in the territory over which he had jurisdiction.

At the local level government was very simple. It was administered by a single magistrate sent down by the central authority, assisted by his staff, who were mostly local personnel of clerical or lower status. This one official would have complete charge over the populace of an entire county. Such a task was possible to perform only because government in those times was not expected to

*This section describes post-Han China in generalized terms.

render services to the people. The magistrate was there to see to the collection and forwarding of taxes, to keep a sharp lookout for subversive activities, to quell any banditry or insurrection, and to try criminal and civil cases. As for the latter, both government and people expected that disputes would be settled whenever possible by the elders of family, lineage, and village—and woe betide unfortunate litigants who resorted to the harsh arbitrament of the magistrate's court. The Chinese attitude was that the peace and order of a district directly reflected the moral character of its magistrate. The saying of Confucius expressed the ideal:

> Lead them with laws and keep them in order by punishments, and the people will avoid [the laws and punishments] without shame. Lead them with moral example and keep them in order by the rules of correct social behavior, and they will have [a sense of] shame and will become [good.][7]

The moral influence of the magistrate was reflected not only in the behavior of men, but even in the reactions of nature. The magistrate, as deputy of the emperor, played the same role of intermediary between human and natural forces in the small territory under his control. The state cults to be maintained by each local capital were prescribed by governmental regulations, and performance of the appropriate rituals was the personal responsibility of the magistrate. The local people, on their part, expected the magistrate to use his official authority on their behalf and to intercede with the appropriate spiritual powers in the event of flood, drought, or pestilence.

The official religious facilities required in every local capital were of three types: memorial halls, of which the Confucian temple was by far the most important; altars; and official cult temples.

The Confucian Temple and Its Rites. The Confucian temple was known in recent centuries as *wen miao,* which may be translated as temple of literature, temple of culture, or, most appropriately, the civil temple. All these translations reflect the meaning of *wen* and the specific place occupied by Confucius and his followers, the scholars or literati, in Chinese culture. For Confucius was the great patron of learning, of the high culture, and consequently of the scholar-bureaucrats who ruled the civil government of China. It is most interesting that these educated elite resisted all efforts to deify their Master and that in a land where it was commonplace to turn men into gods, Confucius remained a human figure. Perhaps he could most aptly be called the spiritual ancestor of the literati.

The Confucian temple was built to the same architectural design as all other temples, generally speaking (see Chapter 4). The main hall contained the spirit tablets of Confucius and four attendant sages: Yen Hui (his favorite disciple), Tzu Ssu (his grandson, and supposed author of *Chung Yung*), Tseng Tzu (another prominent disciple), and Mencius. The tablet of Confucius, which stood in the center of the hall facing the entranceway to the south, was inscribed with the title Confucius still bears: Most Holy Former Master, The Philosopher K'ung. Along the east and west walls of the main hall were the tablets of twelve men honored with the title *che,* the wise. Eleven of these were personal disciples of the Master, while the twelfth was Chu Hsi (A.D. 1130–1200), greatest of the Neo-Confucian philosophers, whose interpretations of the Canon became the orthodoxy of the State. In each of the cloisters forming the east and west sides of the temple compound the tablets of thirty-five eminent Confucians were arranged in order of seniority through the centuries. North of the main hall was a separate building housing the tablets of the ancestors of Confucius for five generations.

The entire complex was thus a memorial hall rather than a palace of gods; it was designed to perpetuate the fame of the greatest Confucians throughout Chinese history. Its resemblance to the ancestral temples of private clans was especially due to the spirit tablets; however, prior to A.D. 1530 the look of the Confucian temple would have been more like that of Buddhist, Taoist, or other cult temples since images were then used instead of spirit tablets.

The sacrifices in the *wen miao* were held twice yearly, in mid-spring and mid-autumn, during the second and eighth lunar months. At the fourth watch (the night was divided into five watches), the sacrifice was offered to the ancestors of Confucius, and at the fifth watch the sacrifice in the main hall commenced. This would be just at dawn. The senior officials of the prefecture were in attendance, the chief celebrant being the magistrate himself. The officials lined the sides of the courtyard below the hall, while in the center six ranks of young students in their traditional costume held long wands tipped with pheasant feathers. In the hall itself, and out on the broad porch, were arranged the sacrificial articles, each in its prescribed vessel. Directly before the high tablet of Confucius was placed a roll of silk, behind it three chalices of wine, behind them three bowls of two kinds of soup; then came two rows of eight vessels, each containing its appropriate viand, and behind these two more rows, each with four dishes. In the next row were the large animals—in the center an ox and to the left and right a pig and a sheep. These were backed by four small candles in their holders, and in the last, or outermost row, stood an incense brazier flanked by large red candles in their holders.

Before each of the four subordinate tablets in the main hall there were similar arrangements of offerings, and the tablets in the cloisters likewise had their sacrifices—all in appropriately descending degrees of elaborateness. The arrays of edibles constituted a banquet for the honored souls, the more sumptuous in quantity and variety giving more honor in accordance with the rank of the spiritual guest.

The beat of drums marked each stage in the ceremonies. An orchestra played an ancient melody in long-drawn-out whole notes, and the ranks of students postured sedately with their wands. A herald cried out instructions for each action, and the chief celebrant and the rest of the officials followed these instructions silently. The celebrant offered incense, dishes of food, and goblets of wine, each offering being accompanied by the kotow and a hymn of praise.

Top, Confucian temple in Taipei on Teachers' Day (birthday of Confucius). The rows of boys on the fore-porch posture very slowly with their feathered wands. *Middle,* musicians performing for service in the *wen-miao;* the man in foreground points to the note to be played. *Bottom,* looking from the altar to the officiants in the Confucian ceremony, the sacrificial animals, and the courtyard beyond.

... The great drum boomed upon the night, the twisted torches of the attendants threw uncertain shadows across the lattice scrolls, and the silk embroideries on the robes of the officials gleamed from the darkness.

The flutes sounded, and the chant rose and fell in strange, long-drawn quavers.

"Pai," [make obeisance] and the officials fell to their knees, bending forward till their heads touched the ground.

"Hsin," [arise] and they were erect again.

Within the hall, the ox lay with his head toward the image [the scene recalls Yuan times] of Confucius. The altar was ablaze with dancing lights, which were reflected from the gilded carving of the enormous canopy above. Figures moved slowly through the hall, the celebrant entered, and the vessels were presented toward the silent statue of the sage, the "Teacher of Ten Thousand Generations." The music was grave and dignified. . . . The dancers struck their attitudes, moving their wands tipped with pheasant feathers in unison as the chant rose and fell. . . .

... It is in reality one of the most impressive rituals that has ever been devised. The silence of the dark hour, the magnificent sweep of the temple lines, with eaves curving up toward the stars, the aged trees standing in the courtyard, and the deep note of the bell, make the scene unforgettable to one who has seen it even in its decay.[8]

The formal prayer read at this service went as follows:

Wei! On K'ang Hsi [reign period 1662–1722] such-and-such a year, month, and day, the official N. of such-and-such a *yamen,* and others, venture to announce to the Most Holy Former Master K'ung Tzu:

Wei! The efficacy of the Master matches that of Heaven and Earth, and his Way excels all others past and present. He revised and wrote the Six Scriptures, he has handed down the model polity of our state for ten thousand generations.

Wei! At this mid-spring (or, mid-autumn), respectfully, with animals and silk, with sweet wine, with vessels of millet and every other kind of offering, in reverent observance of the ancient ritual prescriptions, we spread before thee this divine sacrifice. Accompanying [thee in the reception of the sacrifice] are the Secondary Sages Yen Tzu, Tseng Tzu, Tzu Ssu Tzu, and Meng Tzu.

Deign to receive it![9]

The Altars. The Confucian temple and other, lesser memorial halls served primarily a commemorative and inspirational function, whereas the union of the human and the supernatural, the meshing of this-worldly and other-worldly power, was centered at three altars located in their own compounds. These altars were dedicated respectively to the gods of land and grain, the gods of the mountains and rivers, and the souls of those who had been deprived of their ancestral sacrifices—the bereaved spirits. The origin of the first two groups goes back into Shang times, while the third resulted from native theories of the soul.

A local history of Taiwan describes the altars in the prefectural capital in the early eighteenth century. The altars to the gods of land and grain and to the gods of the mountains and rivers adjoined each other in the same enclosure and were similar in construction. They faced west, were square, measured more than twenty feet each way, were about three feet high, and had three steps on each side. They were bounded by a brick wall having a picket gate on the west. The courtyard between altars and walls was more than twenty feet in width. The total effect, in the words of the history, was that "although it was not completely in accord with the ancient regulations, yet it did not fail to carry on the ancient tradition."[10] The only difference in the two altars was that the land and grain altar had a stone pillar buried in its exact center, one foot one inch square, two feet five inches long, its top bell shaped and protruding.*

The altar to the gods of the mountains and rivers held three tablets: in the center place of honor was the tablet to the *"Shen* (god or spirit) of Wind, Clouds, Thunder, and Rain"; on the left, next in rank, was the tablet of the prefectural *"Shen* of Mountains and Rivers"; and on the right was the tablet of *"Shen* of Walls and Moats"—that is, the spiritual magistrate of the prefecture. All the tablets of the altars were normally kept in the latter's separate temple and were brought to the altars on the occasions of sacrifice. The spiritual magistrate (*ch'eng huang*) played a central role in the official religion of the locality, as the counterpart in the spiritual realm of the living magistrate in this one. He was in fact usually a deceased official thus appointed in his new term by imperial commission. He had charge over the bereaved spirits, who were enjoined to report to him all instances of either good or evil deeds performed by men that would otherwise remain unknown and thus go unrewarded or unpunished. According to regulations, every magistrate upon arrival at a new post was to spend the night prior to formal assumption of his office in the temple of the *ch'eng huang,* purifying himself and praying for the assistance of his spiritual colleague. This procedure was also followed by magistrates baffled by a law case, and numerous instances are recorded of the *ch'eng huang* revealing the solution to his opposite number in a dream.

Official Cults. We have already described the process by which a cult would extend in importance until the government recognized it and bestowed imperial sanction and patronage. Any cult thus recognized and patronized would be included in the official worship to be performed by local officials.

Whatever gods might be on the official roster at any particular time, one was sure to be worshipped: the local earth god. As we know, he was ubiquitous in the folk religion, and of course a deity so close to the lives of all the people could never be omitted from the official cults. As *hou-t'u* we saw him in the third rank of the official pantheon. Whether or not the local histories mention him, it is to be assumed that his shrines are most numerous of all. Every government office had such a shrine, as did every village and city subsection. The local guardian spirit is so essential in the Chinese view that even strictly Buddhist monasteries include such deities under the name *ch'ieh lan.*

In every *yamen* "incense was to be burned [at the local earth god's shrine] on every new and full moon, while those who held official responsibility were to

*Although we eschew conjectural interpretations in this general survey, the phallic character of this stone pillar in the altar to the spirits of land and grain will be apparent, as will the suitability of that symbol to the meaning of the altar.

pray for the welfare of the people."[11] The usual spring and autumn sacrifices given to the gods included offerings to the local earth god. A prayer accompanying the sacrifice was short and simple, but eloquently indicates the deity's important position:

> *Wei!* The efficacy of *shen* extends so far as to transform and sustain, to preserve and protect all [within these] city walls. *Shen* defends the nation and shelters the people, and all we officials rely upon him completely.
> Now, during the mid-spring (or, mid-autumn), we respectfully offer animals and sweet wine in this ordinary sacrifice.
> Deign to accept them![12]

SELECTED READINGS

Yang, C. K., *Religion in Chinese Society.* Berkeley and Los Angeles: University of California Press, 1961; papercover available. Masterly analysis.

Williams, E. T., "The State Religion of China during the Manchu Dynasty," *Journal of the North China Branch, Royal Asiatic Society,* Vol. XLIV, 1913. Good article on the imperial worship.

Huang, K'uei-yen, and J. K. Shryock, "A Collection of Chinese Prayers," *Journal of the American Oriental Society,* Vol. 49, 1929. From an official liturgical manual.

Shryock, John K., *The Origin and Development of the State Cult of Confucius.* New York and London: The Century Co., 1932. Still the only full-scale historical treatment.

Hsiao, Kung-chuan, *Rural China. Imperial Control in the Nineteenth Century.* Seattle: University of Washington Press, 1960; papercover available. See section entitled "Tz'u-ssu: Local Sacrifices," pp. 220–229.

Moule, G. E., "Notes on the *Ting-chi,* or Half-Yearly Sacrifice to Confucius," *Journal of the North China Branch, Royal Asiatic Society,* Vol. XXXIII, 1900–01. Interesting details on the rituals.

Thompson, Laurence G., *The Chinese Way in Religion.* Encino, Calif., and Belmont, Calif.: Dickenson Publishing Company, Inc., 1973. See Part Four: Religion of the State.

Perry, John W., *Lord of the Four Quarters. Myths of the Royal Father.* New York: George Braziller, Inc.; 1966. See pp. 204–218 for treatment of the sacral kingship in China.

6.

The Individual: Buddhism and Taoism

Personal and Institutionalized Religion

In any society there will be persons impelled by one reason or another into the religious vocation. To such persons religion is more than a set of social functions in which they participate simply by virtue of being members of the society. China has had its share of saints and sages, seers and miracle workers, fanatics and pious lay devotees. As in the West this "professional" expression of religion has been largely institutionalized; but in China the professional religious institutions failed to develop temporal power sufficient to give them a major role in secular history, as they did in the West. Any potential threat of the Buddhist institution to the State was ended as early as the ninth century. No Chinese emperor ever went barefoot or with bended knee before a priest of any religion (although some were devout believers in one or another of the religions), and no ecclesiastical sanction was involved in the conferral of Heaven's mandate upon the sovereign. Such political influence as the religious institutions had was either in the form of the individual proclivities of rulers to favor one teaching or another, or in the inspiration they furnished to the activities of insurrectionary secret societies.

In this chapter we shall discuss the three principal forms taken by the personal, voluntary religion in China: Buddhism, Taoism, and the laymen's religion of Buddho-Taoist inspiration. Buddhism and Taoism have, as we have seen, strongly influenced all of Chinese religion; here we wish to characterize them in their own proper selves. Although Taoism antedates Buddhism in China and is a true, native tradition, it will be convenient for us to consider Buddhism first, especially because the so-called religious Taoism reached its mature form only after the introduction of Buddhism at the beginning of the Christian era, and was heavily indebted to it.

Chinese Buddhism

What is Chinese Buddhism? In this brief discussion we can give only the most summary answer. We have to acknowledge at the outset that the historical development of Buddhism in China is as yet very imperfectly known and that study of the literature of Mahāyāna Buddhism is still in its early stage. Here we must ignore the whole prior history of Buddhism in India and preface our outline of the most important religious features of Chinese Buddhism with a single paragraph of background generalities.*

During the long centuries from the beginning of the Later Han dynasty (that is, the beginning of the Christian era) to the middle of the T'ang dynasty (about the eighth century), Indian and Central Asian missionaries came to China, the voluminous literature of Buddhism was translated from Sanskrit into Chinese, and many courageous Chinese pilgrims made the attempt to reach India to study, to collect texts and other sacred objects, and to return with their treasures to their homeland. During the earliest days the Chinese seemed to assume that Buddhist teachings were a sort of variant of Taoism, and it was only with much difficulty that the strange and recondite ideas of the Indian religion became understood in all their tremendous range. Although conservatives never ceased to attack Buddhism as a barbarian religion because of its non-Chinese origin, it captured the intellectual world and dominated Chinese thought until the Neo-Confucian movement of the Sung period (eleventh and twelfth centuries). Its effects on all of Chinese culture were almost incalculable, and although they have yet to receive adequate study by historians, these effects were obvious enough in art and architecture, in literature and drama, in language, in philosophy, and in customs. Such matters lie outside our special concern, and we must turn directly to Chinese Buddhism as religion.

Mahāyāna: The Broad Path. The Chinese, while becoming acquainted with all of the Indian schools, were drawn by decided preference to those upholding Mahāyāna views. The philosophical formulation of Mahāyāna is found in the abstruse treatises of Nāgārjuna and his pupil Aryadeva at a time corresponding to the end of the Han dynasty, and these Indian treatises were translated into Chinese by the great scholar Kumārajīva at the beginning of the fifth century. The work of these Buddhist doctors founded the Mādhyamika, or school of the Middle Way.

In the fourth and fifth centuries Asanga and Vasubandhu, dissatisfied with certain of the Mādhyamika premises, proposed their own revisions to found the Yogācāra, or school of Mere Ideation. Their works were translated into Chinese by the greatest of all the pilgrim-scholars, Hsüan Chuang, in the mid-seventh century. The treatises of these two schools became the "systematic theology" of the whole Mahāyāna movement, resulting in a Buddhism that differed widely from the Buddhism of the Pali texts both in theory and in practice.

The difference in theory centered on the ontological problem. That is to say, if there was no ego, then *what* was it that accumulated and carried on *karma* from one existence to another? What was the relationship of this to the nature of ultimate Reality? (Reincarnation as such was not in question; it was an accepted premise in all of Indian religion.)

The discovery of the Buddha Śakyamuni concerning this ontological prob-

*For full treatment of Buddhism the reader is again referred to *The Buddhist Religion* by Richard H. Robinson in Dickenson's THE RELIGIOUS LIFE OF MAN series.

lem was the law of interdependent causation, expressed in the formula: This being so, that comes to be . . . this ceasing to be, that ceases. In the Buddhism of the Pali texts, which the later Mahāyānists called Hīnayāna, this formula sums up a simple and straightforward doctrine: Existence is caused by the unceasing accumulation of *karma;* existence involves all sorts of suffering; salvation means putting an end to the suffering by putting an end to the accumulation of *karma.* One begins to put an end to the accumulation of *karma* when one realizes that every mental or physical action has its proportionate result and that *karma,* is, in fact, the sum of these results. Our *karma*-producing actions are caused by the delusion that we are *real selves,* that the ego is a *permanent identity*—and therefore this self or ego is dominated by egoistical desires or attachments. It is desire, passionate attachment (or its converse, revulsion and hate), caused by ignorance as to the truth about this so-called self, that shackles us to the ever-revolving wheel of birth-life-death-rebirth, through the continuously replenished motive force of accumulating *karma.* Therefore, the key to release from this wheel is the understanding that there is no self or ego, and consequently that desires and the satisfaction of desires are the illusory products of ignorance.

Although this theory is simple and coherent, the problem of just what the illusory self or ego was, and the relationship of this to ultimate Reality, bothered the analytical minds among later Buddhists, and the answers proposed gave rise to a number of schools. Hīnayāna schools seem to have been more realistic, in the philosophical sense, accepting the existence (at least the temporary existence) of a number of elements and aggregates, which they exhaustively catalogued. The elements, called *dharmas,* included such things as sensation, form, memory, space, and energy. The aggregates, called *skandhas,* included material form and the spiritual items of sensation, ideas, concepts, and understanding. Salvation was attained by realization, or enlightenment, concerning the truth that self or ego was merely a temporary association of these *dharmas* and *skandhas.*

But more profound analysis, most notably by the second century philosopher Nāgārjuna, showed that this Hīnayāna view was still naïve. Not only did self or ego not exist, but the hypothesized *dharmas* and *skandhas* did not exist either. It was just as illogical to posit the existence of numerous components that would come together to form a temporary individual as it was to think that the individual was a thing-in-himself. A thorough-going analysis therefore led to the conclusion that there was literally nothing that had true existence, nothing that could be called a thing-in-itself. The Middle Way of Mādhyamika thus, by a relentless dialectic, destroyed completely the illusion that anything exists. So-called existence was equated with nonexistence. In the Chinese formulation this result was expressed as follows:

> No production and no extinction; no enduring and no cutting off; no unity and no diversity; no arriving and no departing.

Since "existence" and "nonexistence" are in the last analysis identical, a name must be given the true condition. To avoid all characterizations (which would *ipso facto* be false), the name given is Void, or Emptiness (*śūnyatā* in Sanskrit, *k'ung* in Chinese). As one looks at the phenomenal world, one observes the "existence" of "things," and such observation has a relative validity. But when one attains enlightenment one understands that from the level of absolute truth it is equally meaningless to think of any "thing" as either existing or nonexisting. In this paradox the only true statement is that reality is "not this, not this"—and perforce one calls reality *k'ung.* This is strikingly reminiscent of the opening lines of *Lao Tzu* (see Chapter I, p. 6).

The Mādhyamika dialectic destroyed any ultimate "reality" to which one could cling, and in this sense it carried the mission of the Buddha to its logical conclusion. *Śūnyatā* became the central philosophical tenet of East Asian Buddhism. At the same time it provoked a reaction; by its complete denial of any conceivable reality Mādhyamika seemed to go beyond logic and credibility. For this reason Asaṅga and Vasubandhu argued that *thought* at least must exist. Their Yogācāra school took a position similar to the general thesis of philosophical idealism in the West. "Knowledge" was explained on three levels: the illusory "common sense" level; the relative level at which things are conceived as having temporary existence through combination of components; and the true level, which is in fact the same as Mādhyamika. The distinctive feature of the school was its postulation of a "universal storehouse" of thought—a universal consciousness—which is the source of individual consciousness. Such an hypothesis struck most Chinese as fantastic, and, as Chan has pointed out, it did not make much of an impression in Chinese Buddhist circles.[1]

By itself, this profounder philosophical analysis of the Mahāyāna (that is, Mādhyamika) would not have created a form of Buddhism distinctively different from that based on Pali texts. In our typically Western concern with the philosophical aspects of Buddhism, we must always remind ourselves that Buddhism is a religion, not a philosophy. The intellectual work of the Buddhist doctors was not, after all, the seeking of theoretical truth for its own sake; its purpose was to clarify various points concerning the meaning of, and the way to attain, the religious goal of enlightenment. The abstruse writings of these theorists, like the works of Christian theologians, provided the foundation for systematic doctrine, but not the substance of the religious life. Probably only a very few Chinese Buddhists, either in the Saṅgha or lay devotees, ever thoroughly understood or even studied such difficult formulations of doctrine.

More pertinent to Buddhism as a religion is the Mahāyāna development in which Buddha, from the original signification of an enlightened human being, became in fact the equivalent of the Godhead in other religions. A form of docetism interpreted the earthly career of Śakyamuni as a compassionate expedient for the salvation of men, and this same explanation of expedience (*upaya*) became a general feature of the Mahāyāna movement. *Upaya* accounts for the variant teachings of the schools and justifies all the techniques whereby the Buddhist Law brings salvation to sentient beings.

Salvation in the earlier Buddhist teachings had been explained as the hard-won fruit of countless incarnations during which the aspirant disciplined himself to extinguish the passions tying him to the flux of existence. Its goal, called *nirvāṇa,* while never defined by Śakyamuni, seemed to be something negative, in the sense that it was the termination of one's connection with life. *Nirvāṇa* was earned by unremitting striving; it was a personal victory over ignorance. The teachings of Śakyamuni were a signpost, but one had to make one's own way to the goal.

Salvation in the Broad Path of the Mahāyāna was presented on two levels: to the man capable of the highest understanding it was enlightenment as to the Voidness of Reality and thus release from the torments of egoism; to the ordinary man it was pictured as a paradise where, among the most beautiful and uplifting surroundings, the souls of believers heard from the Buddha Himself the words that would bring them to true enlightenment. Moreover, ordinary men were not left to their own feeble resources in the religious quest. Buddha was not just a sage who had left wise teachings for the guidance of his followers; He was an eternally subsisting Being, a Deity, and He actively succored all beings who longed for salvation.

In this great work, according to the Mahāyāna scriptures, Buddha Śakyamuni was assisted by countless buddhas and bodhisattvas. On the highest level the Godhead (or Ultimate Reality, or Void) was of course One and undefinable. But on the relative level, the Principle of Buddha might be conceived as infinitely multiple. At the level where expedience (*upāya*) sought to meet the limitations of popular understanding, the buddhas and bodhisattvas became individualized deities, comprehensible and approachable by the ignorant masses. The bodhisattva, a being who had attained enlightenment and the limitless powers that enabled him to become Buddha, was the specific ideal of Mahāyāna. The individual, personal salvation won by the Hīnayāna *arhat* was denigrated as a selfish, limited ideal, and was contrasted with the Mahāyāna ideal of the saint who —although he had won through to salvation—yet vowed to devote all his religious power to helping others along the way. In the Mahāyāna ordination, the monk therefore took the vow of the bodhisattva.

Monks and Monasteries. Monachism was a distinctive feature of Buddhism from the start. If one sought to follow the prescription of Śakyamuni, that the way to escape the wheel of rebirth and never-ending suffering was to cool the flames of desire into the ashes of nonattachment, one obviously had to leave the world of the home and the society in which desire and attachment were the motivating forces. The followers of the Buddha grew into a vast community, and it was necessary to devise rules for the government of this community. These rules, codified as the *Vinaya,* became one of the major divisions of the early Buddhist Canon. They were believed to have been promulgated by the Buddha himself, and because of this belief they retained binding authority over all the Buddhist monastic communities through the centuries. Thus, the Saṅgha in China was under the same regulations as the Saṅgha everywhere, with only minor differences brought about by local conditions.

One difference was that Chinese monks often did not follow the original Indian tradition of medicancy. The Chinese Saṅgha tended to live in settled fashion, grouped in individual monasteries that were usually supported by landholdings. Their economic base was the income from lands worked by tenant peasants. This more sedentary character of the Chinese Order was perhaps a result of the climatic difference from India, where only during the rainy season were the monks unable to wander freely. In part it would also have resulted from the difference in social traditions, that of China having little place for the wandering mendicant, in contrast to the age-old custom of India. Even more than in India, then, the monastery was in China the center of Buddhist life.

Chinese monasteries varied from huge to tiny, their population numbering hundreds or even thousands in the former case, while the latter would include the hut or cave of the solitary anchorite. Some were famous centers of pilgrimage, noted for great teachers, and honored by the State, while far more were isolated, obscure, and humble. Ideally they were built in places far from the contamination of the dusty world, where the quiet beauties of nature provided an inspirational setting for the religious life. In any Chinese landscape painting we can find one or more such Buddhist (or Taoist) retreats located in the sheltered valleys, amidst soaring peaks, rushing streams, and hoary pines. Not the least of their functions was to serve as hostels during the visits of lay devotees or ordinary citizens seeking temporary refuge from the noise, the strife, and the tensions of society. To all men their doors were open and their simple hospitality freely given. To layman and casual visitor alike they also offered the unaggressive evangelism of their physical arrangements: they were not only monasteries, or homes for the Saṅgha, but also temples, housing the icons of Buddhism that were deities to the simple, and symbols of the Buddhist Truth of Law to the sophisticated.

It would be impossible to know what proportion of the Saṅgha were true seekers after religious salvation and what proportion were members for fortuitous reasons. There is no doubt that many were given by parents in fulfillment of religious vows. There is also no doubt that because of the structure of Chinese society, in which there was no place for unfortunates who for one reason or another had been displaced from their families, the Saṅgha served as a refuge. This "social security" function, while of course bringing into the Saṅgha many who were not religiously motivated, should not be deprecated on that account. It was certainly one aspect of Buddhism that contributed to its survival in the later ages of the Confucian State, as may be indicated by the following remark typifying the attitude of the Confucian literati:

> Buddhist monks and nuns are heretics among the people; yet throughout history they have not been abolished. For by this means the widower and the widow, the childless and the orphan, have available succor to save them from death.[2]

A person often joined the Saṅgha by applying, or being given as a child, to the master of some small temple. Here he would receive training as a novice. A peculiarly Chinese aspect of this practice is that the relationship of master and

Top, Buddhist service. *Middle,* Buddhist service for souls. *Bottom,* newly ordained Buddhist monks bowing as senior officiating monks retire from ceremonies.

novice was often considered the equivalent of the natural father-son relationship. Thus, even in the celibate Buddhist Saṅgha the Chinese family system retained its hold, with monk "families" continuing through many generations.

After preliminary studies the novice would travel to some monastery noted for its great tradition of famous masters, and there he would apply for ordination. Only certain State-approved monasteries were authorized to issue the ordination certificate—which was thus from one point of view a license granted by the imperial government. Ordination involved a longer or shorter period of study and training, and was conferred in three stages. In later times these three stages, each originally requiring extensive preparation, were for practical reasons combined into a three-part ceremony concluded within a period of a few weeks or days. The bodhisattva vows were, as we have indicated, the important ones. These were (1) to lead all beings to salvation, (2) to seek to put an end to all pain and suffering, (3) to study all teachings of the Buddha, (4) to seek to perfect themselves. After pronouncing these vows in impressive rituals supervised by duly authorized senior monks, the candidates were branded by burning incense on their shaven pates, and became *ho-shang,* or full-fledged monks.

The newly ordained monk might either return to his original master to serve in the local temple and eventually to take over its administration; apply for permanent service in the monastery in which he had been ordained; or take to wandering from one monastery to another in order to visit all the holy places throughout the country. Any monk would be accepted for a few days' stay in any monastery upon presenting his ordination certificate. The peripatetic career of such wandering monks is indicated by the picturesque name given to the monastery dormitory in which they were housed: the *yün-shui t'ang,* or clouds and streams hall.

The life of the monk in the monastery was strictly regulated by the *Vinaya,* as we have said, and in addition each monastery had its local administrative routine. Duties were divided into various areas. These usually included study of the canonical literature (one or several sacred texts were often emphasized, according to the particular monastery or master), meditation or yogic concentration, officiation at public or private worship services (especially the soul-masses) upon request, and the daily housekeeping tasks. The more menial chores were performed by lay servants. Government of the monastery was in the hands of the abbott, who was elected by the monks, and his appointed officers. The abbott of an important monastery would be confirmed in office by the State—another indication of its close supervision of religious institutions. The power of the abbot within the monastery was, like that of the senior person in any Chinese institution, paternalistic, and extended to the expulsion of any monk who committed a grave sin or who was incorrigibly nonconformist.

The monastery-temple, although open to visitors and even to long-term guests, was in no sense a church, nor were its resident monks engaged in religious work in the community. As we know, their major contact with the community nearby was in connection with the mortuary rites. The soul-masses might be performed in the home of the deceased or they might be held on the premises of the monastery itself. Occasionally, also, a patron of the monastery might request a lecture or a series of lectures on the Buddhist Law by a renowned scholar-monk, and at such times a congregation of sorts would assemble.

These scholar-monks, called *fa-shih* (or masters of the Law), were the elite among the Saṅgha. They were educated men with special competence in the highly technical literature of the enormous Buddhist Canon, and as such they often commanded great respect at the highest levels of Chinese society. But it is probable that in all ages the rank and file of the Saṅgha were only semiliterate, trained in the *Vinaya* ordinances, taught to perform the necessary rituals, and able to recite by rote a smattering of Chinese versions of the sacred texts and the unintelligible Sanskrit formulas. This is not, of course, to imply that such monks were necessarily inferior in religious attainments. While the Chinese tended to equate scholarship and spiritual caliber, it is by no means certain that such an equation will always balance.

Chinese Buddhist Schools. Most of the Indian Buddhist schools, as represented by their texts, came into China during the first five or six centuries A.D. These schools, whose differences were mostly philosophical, must have presented a perplexing problem to the Chinese, who were not only faced with the difficulty of reconciling conflicting doctrines, but were also unprepared by their own traditions to engage themselves in the sort of speculation that intrigued the Indian mind. In the upshot, what we shall call Chinese Buddhism, as opposed to Indian Buddhism in China, reflected the harmonizing, compromising temper of the Chinese mind, with its interest in practice rather than theory.

This harmonizing, compromising tendency is exemplified in the two great schools called T'ien-t'ai and Hua-yen. Both were founded in the latter part of the sixth century by Chinese masters, and both had as their rationale the thesis that the differences in Buddha's teachings as found in various texts were explainable as expedience, *upaya*. Thus, the Buddha, as a great teacher, understood that different approaches are necessary in order to meet the needs of different people. The task undertaken by the founders of the Chinese schools was to find the order in the myriad scriptures, and to identify the progression of the Buddha's teaching from most elementary to most refined, from simplest to most comprehensive, and thus to see the whole Canon and the various schools as one great system. Kenneth Ch'en has summarized as follows:

> The T'ien-t'ai School represented the Chinese attempt to establish a great eclectic school recognizing all forms of Buddhism. Through its comprehensive and encyclopedic nature it had a place for all the Buddhist scriptures; it considered these scriptures as being gradually revealed by the master when he found that his audience was gradually beginning to understand his message better and better. The school saw no antagonism between the Hīnayāna and Mahāyāna; all sutras were to be accepted as true words of the Buddha if they were considered as being taught during a certain period. The school, however, did believe the *Saddharma [Lotus Sutra]* to contain the

essence of all the teachings, and also taught that all men could become the Buddha, since all possessed the Buddha-nature.[3]

The T'ien-t'ai school's own theoretical standpoint has been called a sort of pantheism: "There is no noumenon besides phenomenon; phenomenon itself is noumenon. . . . All things have no reality and, therefore, are void. But they have temporary existence. They are at the same time mean or middle, that is true state, Thusness."[4] We recognize here the basic Mahāyāna position as formulated in the Mādhyamika treatises of Nāgārjuna. According to T'ien-t'ai, as all beings are of the same Buddha-nature, all are to attain Buddhahood eventually.

The Hua-yen school also arranged the teachings of the Canon in systematic progression, but decided that the pinnacle of the Buddha's thought was found in the *Avatamsaka,* or *Garland Sūtra.* The philosophical conclusions of the Hua-yen were similar to the T'ien-t'ai, but even more universal:

> . . . There is a world of li or ultimate principle*and a world of shih or phenomena, which are perfectly interfused with each other. At the same time each individual phenomenon is also unimpededly identified with every other phenomenon. A totalistic system is thus established, with everything leading to one point, the Buddha, in the center.

> . . . Since all phenomena are manisfestations of one immutable noumenon, they are in perfect harmony with one another, like the different waves of the same water. From the religious point of view everything in the universe, animate and inanimate, are [sic] all representations of the same supreme mind, and can perform the work of the Blessed One.[5]

It will be seen that the establishment of these two Chinese schools, far from compounding the sectarian division of Buddhism, in fact worked for ecumenism. Neither claimed a monopoly of truth, and both acknowledged the necessity of various teachings to suit various needs. They did try to define the highest truth, but they recognized the value and the validity of what they considered to be only relative truth.

The emphasis of the foregoing schools was on the universality of Buddhist salvation, based upon the philosophical tenet that all creation shares in the Buddha-nature. But in their scholastic work of systematizing the order of the Canon they did not yet arrive at a practical way of fully implementing this universal salvation. That way was developed by a third Chinese school, the Ching-t'u, or Pure Land. This school held that all men were capable of salvation, and not just the few fortunate enough to be able to devote their whole lives to religion in the Sangha. The basis for this belief was, in the first place, the universal Buddha-nature, and, in the second place, the assertions in certain scriptures, notably the *Lotus Sūtra,* and the *Larger* and *Smaller Sukhāvatī-Vyūha Sūtras* (translated in Chinese as *Sutra of Limitless Longevity*), that unlimited mercy was available to the cry of faith. Specifically, the Pure Land was the kingdom estab-

*This *li* is a different word from the *li* meaning the norm of social behavior.

lished by the Bodhisattva Dharmākara in fulfillment of his vows upon attainment
of Buddhahood as Amitābha:

> When I have become a Buddha
> May my country be the highest,
> Its people rare and excellent,
> Its field-of-Truth superlative,
> The land as good as Nirvāna,
> Matchless and incomparable.
> Then in pity and compassion
> I will liberate all beings.
> Men from ten quarters who, reborn,
> Their hearts rejoicing and unstained,
> Have arrived inside my country
> Will dwell in peace and happiness.[6]

Entry into this paradise of Buddha Amitābha was won by devotion to the
Buddha and by meritorious deeds, but above all (and, in some interpretations,
exclusively) by faith. The arduous practices of self-discipline, study, and yogic
concentration were not required. The pietistic form of Buddhism, carrying the
conception of the boundless compassion of the Savior to the logical extreme, went
so far as to declare that the most sinful of men, if struck with contrition at the
moment of death and able to call the name of the Savior only once in genuine
faith, would be taken to the Western Paradise (as Amitābha's kingdom was
called). The practice of this school reduced itself to the reaffirmation of faith
through frequent repetition of the sacred formula, *Nanmo Amit'o Fo,* Hail to
Amitābha Buddha! An important feature of the pietistic school was the evolution
of the Bodhisattva Avalokiteśvara, the principal helper of Amitābha, into the
most prominent deity not only of Ching-t'u, but of the folk religion as well. As
we saw in our discussion of the major deities of Taiwan (see Chapter 4), Avalokiteśvara is called Kuan-yin in Chinese, and has become a compassionate mother-
figure in this folk religion.

It is easy to see why the Pure Land became the most popular school of
Chinese Buddhism. It is perhaps not so easy to see why the fourth of the great
Chinese schools gained its dominant position. This was the school called Ch'an
(a Chinese transliteration of the Sanskrit *dhyāna,* meaning yogic concentration),
so suddenly and strangely fashionable in the West these days under its Japanese
pronunciation and color, Zen. Like Ching-t'u, Ch'an was a reaction against the
scholastic and formalistic preoccupations of other Buddhist schools, but unlike
Ching-t'u Ch'an offered no "easy road" to salvation through faith.

In one sense Ch'an was a return to the sort of Buddhism the Mahāyāna had
deplored in Hīnayāna schools: it taught that salvation was enlightenment concerning the true nature of Reality or Void (that is, the Mādhyamika *śūnyatā*),
but that it had to be fought for and won in the Hīnayāna way, through personal
striving. The great mission of Ch'an was to reiterate the message so often pro-

claimed by Śakyamuni—namely, that the problem was suffering and that the only goal was the elimination of suffering. In other words, philosophy was not the essence of religion, scripture reading was not the method of religion, and there were no other powers (buddhas and bodhisattvas) "out there" to help the sufferer escape his predicament. Further, good deeds in themselves—while admirable and necessary—had nothing to do with achieving enlightenment, and no amount of ritual or magic could contribute an iota to salvation.

The adherents of Ch'an sought to cut directly through to the solution by means of the meditational techniques that would lead to the realization of truth, and in this also they may be said to be following the traditional account of the attainment of enlightenment by Śakyamuni. The tenets of Ch'an were summed up in a typically laconic Chinese formula:

> By mind transmitting to mind. No establishment of the written word. Transmission [of the teachings of the school] outside of the [orthodox] religion. Pointing directly to the human mind, and seeing the innate nature, one becomes Buddha: this mind is already Buddha.[7]

Ch'an was thus a method, or one might say *the* method, to attain enlightenment, and its utter frankness in exposing the futility of all the other methods has sometimes led to accusations that it is actually not Buddhism at all. But as we have pointed out, not only was Ch'an in a real sense a return to the basic Buddhism of the Founder, but the Ch'an method was practiced to some extent in all schools. Besides, enlightenment was by no means the sole goal of Buddhism as a religion, and Ch'an monks led the same life of discipline, asceticism, and virtue as all their fellows in the Sangha. In the end, the centality of the Ch'an technique was accepted in Chinese Buddhism, and it assumed the leading position among the Sangha schools.

Having briefly described the major Chinese schools, we should emphasize that Chinese Buddhism is after all essentially nonsectarian. The most striking thing about these Chinese schools is not their individualism, but their harmonization. If to the four schools discussed above we add the Indian Vinaya school (called Lü in Chinese), which stressed the task of living up to the code enacted by Śakyamuni for cenobitic life and was thus neither a philosophical school nor a school stressing particular techniques of enlightenment, we may see Chinese Buddhism as a whole in the following terms. The religious life has various requirements, even though one school may emphasize one aspect over another. These requirements are (1) intellectual understanding, or Buddhist wisdom (T'ien-t'ai and Hua-yen); (2) faith (Ching-t'u); (3) meditation, or inner striving to enlightenment concerning *śūnyatā* (Ch'an); and (4) the life lived in moral self-control under the discipline of the rules given by the Buddha Himself (Lü). Thus, in the Chinese view there was no real incongruity in the fact that adherents and practices of several schools were found under the same roof in many monasteries. It should be emphasized that "school Buddhism" was in China of concern only to the professional religious, and that the ordinary Chinese would neither know nor care about the such distinctions.

Religious Taoism

Origins. We now know that the premise of Buddhism is that life is suffering, that suffering arises from desires or passions, and that desires or passions arise from the erroneous conviction that the ego exists. In Mahāyāna the religious quest leads to enlightenment not only as to the nonexistence of ego, but also as to the illusory condition of all the phenomenal world. When one has attained enlightenment, one is fully aware of the transcendental character of ultimate Reality, one is "dead" to the desires of this world, and one attains the wisdom and compassion of the bodhisattva.

In contrast, the premise of religious Taoism is that life is good and to be enjoyed. The individual self is not set apart from the rest of nature, but is, like all things, a product of *yin* and *yang* as the operational processes of *tao*. Neither the ego nor the rest of the phenomenal world is illusory—both are completely real. *The religious quest is for liberation of the spiritual element of the ego from physical limitations, so that it may enjoy immortality or at least longevity.* In other words, the goal is the triumph of the *yang* over *yin*. When one has attained this liberation, this triumph, one may choose either to remain in the physical body to enjoy mundane pleasures or to wander freely in the realm of space, to visit or dwell in one of the fabled abodes of the immortals.

It may seem difficult to reconcile this religious Taoism with the whole purport of the classic Taoist texts *Lao Tzu* (*Tao Te Ching*) and *Chuang Tzu*. And yet, although the authors of these profoundly philosophical works would certainly have been bemused by the theories and practices of the religion that later claimed them as founders, it is, in fact, easy to find in their writings numerous passages that lend themselves to mystical and even esoteric interpretations. A literal, as opposed to a symbolic or poetic reading, could find both the goal of immortality and some techniques for attaining it in such passages as the following:

> He who does not lose his place (with Tao) will endure.
> He who dies but does not really perish enjoys long life.[8]

> I have heard that one who is a good preserver of his life
> will not meet tigers or wild buffaloes,
> And in fighting will not try to escape from weapons of war.
> The wild buffalo cannot butt its horns against him,
> The tiger cannot fasten its claws in him,
> And weapons of war cannot thrust their blades into him,
> And for what reason?
> Because in him there is no room for death.[9]

> Attain complete vacuity.
> Maintain steadfast quietude.[10]

> Close the mouth.
> Shut the doors.
> Blunt the sharpness.

Untie the tangles.
Soften the light.
Become one with the dusty world.
This is called profound identification.[11]

Lieh Tzu could ride the wind and go soaring around with cool
and breezy skill . . .[12]

. . . there is a Holy Man living on faraway Ku-she Mountain, with skin like ice or
snow, and gentle and shy like a young girl. He doesn't eat the five grains, but sucks
the wind, drinks the dew, climbs up on the clouds and mist, rides a flying dragon,
and wanders beyond the four seas. By concentrating his spirit, he can protect creatures from sickness and plague and make the harvest plentiful. . . .[13]

Master Lieh Tzu said to the Barrier Keeper Yin, "The Perfect Man can walk under
water without choking, can tread on fire without being burned, and can travel above
the ten thousand things (i.e., everything in the world) without being frightened. May
I ask how he manages this?"

The Barrier Keeper Yin replied, "This is because he guards the pure
breath. . . ."[14]

The breaths of the true man (like the Perfect Man, this denotes the Taoist master)
come from his heels, while men generally breathe from their throats.[15]

The historical relationship between this sort of thinking as found in the first
Taoist philosophers and the formulation of specific techniques for achieving the
goals at which it hinted is obscure. The goal itself must, of course, be as old as
mankind, but the kinds of practices characteristic of the religious Taoist system
in China were perhaps developed no earlier than three to four centuries B.C. These
practices have been divided into two inclusive categories: the first was called
"outer elixir" (*wai-tan*); this involved the concoction of a drug of immortality.
The second was called "inner elixir" (*nei-tan*); this was the refining by various
means of the spiritual essence within the body in order to liberate this spiritual
essence from its physical shackles.

Wai-tan. The search for a magical elixir, known in the West in later times as
alchemy, began in China. Comparison of theories and procedures of the Chinese
and European varieties of alchemy suggests the indirect derivation of the European from the Chinese. But there was a basic difference of emphasis in the
alchemy in the two civilizations. In China the primary motivation was the desire
to attain immortality, whereas in the West it was the hope of obtaining gold from
base metal.

The earliest literary reference to the elixir is found in the first great history
of China, written by Ssu-ma Ch'ien* in the mid-second century B.C.:

At this time [133 B.C.] Li Shao-jün was also received in audience by Emperor [Wu],
because, by worshipping the Stove and by a method of [not eating] grain [products],
he said he knew how to avoid old age. . . .

*Double surname hyphenated: Ssu-ma.

[Li] Shao-jün spoke to the Emperor, saying 'You should worship the Stove and then you can make [spiritual] beings present themselves; when [spiritual] beings have presented themselves, cinnabar powder can be metamorphosed into gold . . .; when this gold has been made, it can be used for vessels for drinking and eating, and will increase the length of your life; when the length of your life has been increased, the immortals of Peng-lai in the midst of the ocean can thereupon be given audience; when they have been given audience, by [making the sacrifices] *feng* and *shan* you will never die. The Yellow Lord† did this. Your subject has traveled on the ocean and had an audience with Master An-chi. Master An-chi fed your servant jujubes as large as melons. Master An-chi is an immortal who is in communication with those on [the isle of] Peng-lai. When it suits him, he appears to people, and when it does not suit him, he remains hidden.

Whereupon the Son of Heaven [Emperor Wu], for the first time worshipped the Stove in person, sent gentlemen [possessors] of recipes . . . out into the ocean to seek for Master An-chi and similar [beings from the isle of] Peng-lai, and paid attention to metamorphosing powdered cinnabar and potions of various drugs into gold. . . .[16]

The activities of the alchemists were of direct concern to the State, which was anxious to prevent counterfeiting of gold money. For this reason, such activities were proscribed on penalty of public execution. The alchemists, therefore, to avoid prosecution and to protect an esoteric lore, kept their operations secretive, relaying their formulas orally or writing them down in a language so occult and obscure that none but initiates could find them intelligible. One rare text dating from the mid-second century A.D. contains the following explanation of the elixir theory:

Tan-sha (Red Sand, cinnabar, mercury sulfide) is of wood and will combine with gold (metal). Gold (metal) and water live together; wood and fire keep one another company. [In the beginning] these four were in a confused state. They came to be classified as Tigers and Dragons. The numbers for the Dragons, which are *yang* (positive, male), are odd, and those for the Tigers, which are *yin* (negative, female) are even.

The blue liver is the father and the white lungs is the mother. The red heart is the daughter, the yellow spleen is the grandfather, and the black kidneys are the son. The son is the beginning of the *wu-hsing* (the Five Elements). The *three* things are of the same family and they all are of the ordinal numbers *Wu* and *Chi*. . . .[17]

Another passage from the same work pictures the alchemist at work with his ingredients in the cauldron and explains the efficacy of the elixir:

Circumference three-five, diameter one tenth of an inch, mouth four-eight, two inches, length one and two-tenths feet, and thickness equal throughout. With its belly properly set, it is to be warmed up gradually. *Yin* (negativeness) is above and *yang* (positiveness) runs below. The ends are strongly heated and the middle mildly warmed. Start with seventy, and with thirty, and two hundred and sixty. There should be thorough mixing.

†The mythical Emperor Huang Ti.

The *yin* . . . fire is white and produces the *huang-ya* (Yellow Sprout) from the lead. Two-seven gathers to bring forth the man. When the brain [head] is properly tended for the required length of time, one will certainly attain the miracle. The offspring, living securely in the center, plies back and forth without coming out of doors. By degrees he grows up and is endowed with a pure nature. He goes back to the one to return to his origin.

Respectful care should be accorded, as by a subject to his ruler. To keep up the work for a year is indeed a strenuous task. There should be strict protection, so as not to get lost. The Way is long and obscurely mystical, at the end of which the *Ch'ien* (positiveness, male) and the *K'un* (negativeness, female) come together. The taking of so small a quantity of it as would cover the edge of a knife or spatula will be enough to confer tranquility on the *hun-p'o* (man's animal spirit), give him immortality, and enable him to live in the village of the immortals.

. . . Careful reflection is in order, but no discussion with others should take place. The secret should be carefully guarded and no writing should be done for its conveyance.

When the aspirant is accomplished, he will ride on the white crane and the scaled dragon to pay respects to the Immortal Ruler in the Supreme Void. There he will be given the decorated diploma which entitles him to the name of a *Chên-jên* (True Man).[18]

Had alchemy been no more than a technique for producing the elixir, it could be considered as simply proto-science and not as religion; but in fact the adepts of this technique were never simply experimenters with material substances. The major treatise of the alchemical school, written by one Ko Hung (253–333?) under the pen-name Pao P'u Tzu, or the Master Who Cherishes Simplicity, contains many specifications such as the following:

The rules of immortality demand an earnest desire for quietness, loneliness, non-activity and forgetfulness of one's own body.

The rules of immortality require that one extend his love to the creeping worm and do no harm to beings with the life-fluid. . . .

The rules of immortality require that one entirely abstain from flesh, give up cereals and purify one's interior.

The rules of immortality demand universal love for the whole world, that one regard one's neighbor as one's own self.[19]

As in all religions there is a moral imperative in this search for immortality through alchemy:

He who aspires after immortality should, above all, regard as his main duties: loyalty, filial piety, friendship, obedience, goodness, fidelity (all good Confucian virtues). If one does not lead a virtuous life but exercises himself only in magical tricks, he can by no means attain long life. If one does evil, should this be of a grave nature, the god of the fate would take off one chi (300 days, according to translator's note), and for a small sin he would take off a suan (three days) of one's life. . . .

> If the number of good actions is not yet completed, he will have no profit from them, although he takes the elixir of immortality. . . .[20]

The life to be led by the aspirant is described by the same authority:

> . . . This Way is of utmost importance. You must teach it only to those who are wise and virtuous. . . . Whoever receives this instruction, must as a pledge throw a golden effigy of a man and of a fish into a river which flows eastwards. He must smear on his mouth the blood of a victim to pledge allegiance to the cause. . . . One must compound the cinnabar in a famous mountain, uninhabited by human beings, in the company of not more than three persons. First, one must fast for a hundred days, washing and bathing in water mixed with five odoriferous substances and thus effect absolute purity. Avoid strictly proximity to filthy things and observe isolation from the vulgar crowd. Furthermore, disbelievers of the Way should not be given any information, for they would slander and spoil the elixir, and thus the Medicine will fail. . . .[21]

Nei-tan. The quest for the elixir continued on for centuries, becoming increasingly conceived more in spiritual than in physical terms. This development is summed up by Waley, who calls *nei-tan* "esoteric alchemy":

> . . . *Exoteric alchemy* [i.e., *wai-tan*] . . . uses as its ingredients the tangible substances mercury, lead, cinnabar and so on . . . [whereas] *esoteric alchemy* . . . uses only the "souls" of these substances. . . . Presently a fresh step is made. These transcendental metals are identified with various parts of the human body, and alchemy comes to mean in China . . . a system of mental and physical re-education. This process is complete in the *Treatise on the Dragon and Tiger* (lead and mercury) of Su Tung-p'o, written *c.* 1100: "The dragon is mercury. He is the semen and the blood. He issues from the kidneys and is stored in the liver. His sign is the trigram *k'an.* The tiger is lead. He is breath and bodily strength. He issues from the mind and the lungs bear him. His sign is the trigram *li.* When the mind is moved, then the breath and strength act with it. When the kidneys are flushed then semen and blood flow with them."
>
> In the thirteenth century alchemy (if it may still so be called) no less than Confucianism is permeated by the teachings of the Buddhist Meditation Sect [i.e., Ch'an]. The chief exponent of the Buddhicized Taoism is Ko Ch'ang-kêng, also known as Po Yü-chuan. In his treatise . . . he describes three methods of esoteric alchemy: (1) the body supplies the element lead; the heart, the element mercury. Concentration supplies the necessary liquid; the sparks of intelligence, the necessary fire. "By this means a gestation usually demanding ten months may be brought to ripeness in the twinkling of an eye."
>
> . . . (2) The second method is: The breath supplies the element lead, the soul [*shen*] supplies the element mercury. The cyclic sign [*wu*] "horse" supplies fire; the cyclic sign [*tzu*] "rat" supplies water.
>
> (3) the semen supplies the element lead. The blood supplies mercury; the kidneys supply water; the mind supplies fire.
>
> "To the above it may be objected," continues Ko Ch'ang-kêng, "that this is practically the same as the method of the Zen Buddhist. To this I reply that under Heaven there are no two Ways, and that the Wise are ever of the same heart."[22]

Although *wai-tan,* an alchemy of substances, thus becomes more and more a technique for cultivating the "inner chemistry" of the body, it must not be assumed that this latter was historically an outgrowth of the former. On the contrary, as several of the excerpts quoted above from *Lao Tzu* and *Chuang Tzu* show, inner cultivation was already a feature of ancient Taoist philosophy. From these hints the later adepts of religious Taoism developed a variety of yoga, based upon a theory that may be called "spiritual physiology." This in turn formed the foundation for the proto-science of traditional Chinese medicine. The objective of Taoist yoga was, as we have said, liberation of the *yang* soul (that is, the *shen*) from the hindrances of the *yin,* or gross physical body, and thus it was in fact a development of the ancient concepts. That is to say, it had always been presumed that such a liberation was accomplished by death; but the religious Taoists believed it could be accomplished in this very life.

In the spiritual physiology of religious Taoism the life force was identified with such obviously vital components as breath, blood, and semen. To preserve life, these components must be conserved, and the obstructions to their continuing nourishment of the *shen* must be reduced and finally eliminated. The peculiarity about the religious Taoist notion of breath was that it was not merely inhalation and exhalation of an exterior substance, but that it was a progressive "using up" of the allotment of life-spirit with which one was born. Taoist yoga therefore endeavored to conserve the breath. In the same way exhaustion of the semen was equivalent to exhaustion of the life-spirit; therefore adepts used a technique to retain it instead of ejaculating it during the sexual act. Not only did this prevent exhaustion of the life-spirit, but the method of retention was positively beneficial as well. It was believed that pressure on the urethra at the moment of ejaculation forced the semen back up through the spinal passage to the brain, where it nourished the "Field of Cinnabar" supposed to be located there. Through this circulation of the semen (as of the breath) throughout the various passages and organs predicated by Taoist physiological and anatomical theory, the practitioner was continually rejuvenated.

The same purpose lay behind the various gymnastic routines of Taoist devotees, some of which have been widely adopted in East Asia. The so-called Chinese boxing (*t'ai-chi ch'üan*), a slow-motion ballet performed by countless men and women every morning in China, is like the setting-up exercises used in the West. Its rationale, however, is that just described. Such Taoist gymnastics, when combined with the injunctions of Lao Tzu to be nonassertive, "weak like water," and so forth, further led to techniques of bodily combat that have recently become popular among some Westerners, particularly the "yielding way" (*jou-tao* in Chinese, or *jūdō* in Japanese).

The Taoist adept attempted to reduce his intake of food as far as possible, because the consumption of food merely contributed to maintenance of the physical body and produced excreta that clogged the various interior passages, which were to be kept open wide for circulation of the life-forces. Even cereals were to be avoided because the body was inhabited by maleficent spirits (*kuei*) who were nourished by cereals.

The notion of the body being inhabited by both beneficent and malevolent spirits was further extended to the conception of the body as a microcosm corresponding to the macrocosm of the universe. Such an imaginative conception might have had its origin, at least in part, in certain passages of *Chuang Tzu*, where the relativity of things is most powerfully delineated:

> ... In all the world, there is nothing greater than the tip of an autumn hair; Mount T'ai is small. Neither is there any one who was longer lived than a child cut off in its infancy; P'eng Tsu [the "Chinese Methuselah"] himself died young. The universe came into being with us together; with us, all things are one. ...[23]

However, the same sort of thinking was stimulated by the paradoxes beloved of the philosophers of the sophist type who flourished in the fourth and third centuries B.C. And even in the more socially oriented thought of Mencius one finds this curious passage: "The ten thousand things (that is, all things) are complete within us."[24]

At the highest level, among Taoists of superior intellectual and spiritual attainments, the religious quest led not only to the goal of immortality but to a mystical absorption in *tao* itself. While the meditational techniques of Taoism were strongly influenced by Buddhism in later times, ultimately resulting in the Buddho-Taoist techniques of Ch'an, it seems certain that some form of meditation was already practiced in China long before the arrival of the Indian religion. What is hinted at in *Lao Tzu* seems to become explicit in *Chuang Tzu:*

> Nan Kuo Tzu Ch'i sat leaning on a table. He looked to heaven and breathed gently, seeming to be in a trance, and unconscious of his body.
>
> Yen Ch'êng Tzû Yu, who was in attendance on him, said: "What is this? Can the body become thus like dry wood, and the mind like dead ashes? The man leaning on the table is not he who was here before."[25]

> You have heard of the knowledge that knows, but you have never heard of the knowledge that does not know. Look into that closed room, the empty chamber where brightness is born! Fortune and blessing gather where there is stillness. ... Let your ears and eyes communicate with what is inside, and put mind and knowledge on the outside. Then even gods and spirits will come to dwell, not to speak of men ...[26]

> ... I kept on telling him; after three days, he began to be able to disregard all worldly matters. After his having disregarded all worldly matters, I kept on telling him; after seven days, he began to be able to disregard all external things. After his having disregarded all external things, I kept on telling him; after nine days, he began to be able to disregard his own existence. Having disregarded his own existence he was enlightened. Having become enlightened, he was then able to gain the vision of the One. Having the vision of the One, he then was able to transcend the distinction of past and present. Having transcended the distinction of past and present, he was then able to enter the realm where life and death are no more. ...[27]

Formalized Taoism. If Taoism was to meet the challenge of the highly developed religion imported from India, it had to be institutionalized and develop its own corpus of sacred writings, its own liturgy, its own pantheon. Modeling itself on Buddhism, therefore, it formed monastic communities, produced a canon, and created an immense pantheon. The Taoist monks led a life similar to that of their Buddhist rivals, although not usually as ascetic. As for the Taoist Canon (*Tao Tsang*), it grew through the centuries until by the twelfth century, when it was first printed, it filled 5,481 Chinese-style, paper-bound volumes. The Taoist pantheon embraced the entire range of deities in the popular religion, and it is this which led to the common confusion of what are basically two different religious phenomena—Taoism and popular cult religion. Confusion of the two was furthered by the tendency for the more specifically Taoist beliefs and practices to merge with the ancient and always prevalent magic and shamanism, and for the practitioners of the latter to call themselves Taoists.

As in every religion, there was a sectarian development in Taoism. So little is as yet known of this development that it would be futile to attempt any discussion of it here. We may note that in broadest terms there were so-called "northern" and "southern" schools. The latter was the earliest organized movement, its origin being well documented in the historical records of the Later Han dynasty. Its founder was Chang Ling, or Chang Tao-ling, who lived in the second century A.D., and who became known as the "heavenly master" (*t'ien shih*). Although historically speaking the line of descent is very much broken, the southern school still claims a "heavenly master" Chang as its leader. At certain times the special position of this leader has been given recognition by the State —not as an indication of any particular doctrinal authority, but because there seemed to be sufficient organizational prestige attached by the southern school to this leader that it was convenient for the State to fix on him responsibilities for activities of the Taoists.[28] The so-called northern school, usually referred to by its designation "Perfect Truth," is reputedly the more strict and ascetic of the two. Its professional religious "leave the home," abstain from alcohol and those edibles forbidden to fasters (that is, *hun,* for which see Chapter 5, p. 71), and take in novices for training. The southern monks, on the contrary, may indulge in liquor and meat when not observing special fasts, may remain as householders, and acknowledge the special position of the "heavenly master."

It must not be supposed that there has ever been any real overall organization of a Taoist "church." Like Buddhist monasteries and temples, the Taoist institutions were independent units whose government was in the hands of their abbotts. The State did maintain careful surveillance of these institutions, primarily through the system of ordination certificates, as in the case of the Buddhist clergy. The title of "Pope" given by Western writers to the "heavenly master" of the southern school is a fanciful comparison. He had a certain amount of prestige, but only minimal institutional power.

Within the northern and southern schools there were many sects or lines of transmission from master to pupil (*p'ai*). These differed in various respects, but all remained within the general framework of the *wai-tan, nei-tan,* and mixed-in popular religion. One Chinese source lists eighty-six of these sects, but from what little study has been made it seems unlikely that there are differences significant enough to set them apart from one another in the way that Buddhist schools have been distinguished. And as in the case of Buddhism, the sectarian distinctions— as indeed the whole complex of practices in *wai-tan* and *nei tan*—were matters of concern only to the professional religious, and certainly beyond the ken of lay people.

Laymen's Religion of Buddho-Taoist Inspiration

General Characteristics. The number of persons of pious inclinations who were able to "leave the home" and take up the life of the professional religious was, of course, always small in China. For a very much larger number, religious devotions practiced privately in the home or in the company of other like-minded householders constituted the only practicable mode of satisfying personal needs. Because the organized religions with which the Chinese were familiar were Buddhism and Taoism, the laymen's religion was inevitably modeled upon those religions—including of course the adaptations derived from folk religion. In addition, there was the ancestral cult and all the related traditions deriving authority from the Confucian Canon.

It will not be necessary to spell out in detail the characteristics of the laymen's religion, since we have already studied its ingredients. It is apparent that the degree and sincerity with which laymen would privately follow those Buddhist and Taoist practices which appealed to them would vary from individual to individual. Some, particularly among the old (and, it is often claimed, most particularly among older women), who had both less social responsibility and more urgent concern because of the imminence of death, would go so far as to retire completely from normal life and almost become hermits. They would spend the better part of their days in praying, chanting sacred texts, worshipping their favorite icons, and in general trying to cultivate a sanctity certainly equal in fervor to that of the professional religious themselves. Others, with less leisure and more worldly responsibilities, would try to accumulate merit through good deeds and would give moral and economic support to the Buddhist and Taoist institutions. Still others might devote themselves primarily to yogic meditation during a few hours of the day, as much perhaps for health and longevity as for strictly religious purposes. A common feature of the laymen's life was adoption of a vegetarian diet in accordance with the widely accepted belief that all life was sacred, and the killing of animals a grave offense that accumulated "bad *karma.*"

Religious Societies. Laymen frequently banded together in religious societies. Some of these had specific purposes such as building up a joint fund to support group pilgrimages to famous holy mountains. Some were cultish in nature, growing up around the charismatic personality of some self-proclaimed seer or messiah. Such cults were undoubtedly widespread in China, but, because of their unorthodox beliefs (by official Confucian standards) and their secretive nature they have been very little studied. Those which developed from local, purely religious groups into full-fledged movements combining religious fervor with insurrectionist political aims have been given some attention by historians. One, commonly called the Triad Society or the Hung League, has been thoroughly investigated by European scholars and by civil and police authorities as well, because of its political and criminal activities among overseas Chinese in Western colonial areas. The religious element was fundamental to the Yellow Turban movement at the end of the Later Han dynasty (late second century A.D.), in the activities of the White Lotus Society during Ming and Ch'ing times, and in the great Taiping Rebellion of the mid-nineteenth century, but was, in the end, subordinated to economic and political drives. This tendency to change from religious to secular aims makes the terms "religious society" and "secret society" almost synonymous, a fact that is explained by the polity of traditional China.

In this polity there were few institutions standing between the State and the lineage with its families. Those which did exist, such as local communities, guilds, and the Buddhist and Taoist monasteries, functioned only with the permission of the State and were always responsible to the State. The imperial government interfered as little as possible with existing institutions, but the institutional leaders were answerable for the behavior of members; and the government always held in reserve its absolute authority to intervene as it might see fit.

Any group of persons coming together privately to hold meetings, to celebrate rites and ceremonies, and to promote variant beliefs and practices was automatically suspect in the eyes of the State. Such *sub rosa* organizations were guilty of heresy in official eyes, and worse than heresy was the presumption that the actual motives of an extra-legal group were revolutionary. In fact, in this vast country, poorly connected by arteries of transportation, where premodern communications were measured in days, weeks, or even months, a revolutionary movement could develop from a small band of conspirators into a formidable mass uprising before the government could suppress it—or even before knowledge of its existence could reach the distant capital. For this reason, even the most innocuous and purely religious cults or sects were forced underground, and when uncovered were usually ruthlessly persecuted by the State. It would be difficult, if not impossible, to draw real distinctions between the truly religious and the socioeconomic and political considerations that underlay formation of the innumerable secret societies of China.

What must be asserted, however, is that religious need, faith, and sincerity were primary factors leading to the participation in such societies of countless millions of people. That this religious fervor was in many cases coupled with other motives need not cause us to doubt this fact. To use a well-known (if atypically fanatical) group as an example, the so-called Boxers who were utilized by the Manchu Court as a last, desperate measure against the foreign powers at the turn of the twentieth century certainly had real faith in the religious talismans which they were assured would protect them from the bullets of the foreigners' guns. Furthermore, while certain of the secret societies had a long history of political subversion and even of criminal operations, we must not therefore conclude that such was the character of religious societies in general. Given the compulsion of circumstances—tyrannical misgovernment, natural disasters that drove the peasants to the wall—the secret societies could of course easily serve as catalysts for revolt. But undoubtedly the great majority of the societies owed their origin, and appealed by their activities, to the universal human longing for spiritual salvation. Most of them were very small local organizations and hence completely unknown and unrecorded, quite unlike the societies that spread throughout provinces and the whole empire and became notorious as dangerous enemies of the regime.

As for the religious teachings of these societies, they ranged from lay devotees' vows of Buddhism or Taoism to the most novel and ludicrous rantings of self-proclaimed prophets. One may compare these teachings with the range of choice open to the layman in the West, who may adhere to an old, established, conservative sect, may be caught up in the emotionalism of a fundamentalist revival, or may be drawn to the peculiar doctrines of an extremist cult. It is perhaps above all the existence of such a variety of religious activities among the peasant masses which effectively refutes the strange stereotype of the Chinese as a "religiously indifferent" or even an "irreligious" people.

SELECTED READINGS

BUDDHISM

Blofeld, John, *The Jewel in the Lotus: An Outline of Present Day Buddhism in China.* London: The Buddhist Society, 1948. Best introduction.

Hodous, Lewis, *Buddhism and Buddhists in China.* New York: The MacMillan Co., 1924. Another good introduction.

Johnston, Reginald F., *Buddhist China.* London: John Murray, Ltd., 1913. Many interesting comparisons of Chinese Buddhism with non-Chinese religions. Good on pilgrimages; good snapshots.

Prip-Møller, J., *Chinese Buddhist Monasteries: Their Plan and Its Function as a Setting for Buddhist Monastic Life.* New York: Oxford University Press, Inc., 1937; reprinted by Hong Kong University Press, 1967. Monumental and masterly study by architect-sinologist. A thorough, authoritative exposition of all aspects of Buddhist monachism in China, illustrated with 365 plates, plans, and elevations.

Blofeld, John, *The Wheel of Life.* London: Rider & Company, 1959; papercover, Berkeley, Calif; Shambala Publications. Autobiography of a Western Buddhist who spent many years of his religious quest in China.

Ch'en, Kenneth K. S., *Buddhism in China: A Historical Survey;* papercover available. Princeton, N.J.: Princeton University Press, 1964. Treats Buddhism primarily from the institutional point of view; lucid and nontechnical.

Ch'en, Kenneth K. S., *The Chinese Transformation of Buddhism.* Princeton, N.J.: Princeton University Press, 1973; papercover available. The theme is the Sinification of

Buddhism. Mainly an analysis of Buddhist influences in Chinese culture at their height during the T'ang dynasty. By a leading scholar; written in an easily-flowing, nontechnical style.

Davidson, J. LeRoy. *The Lotus Sutra in Chinese Art.* New Haven, Conn.: Yale University Press, 1954. Remarkable study of the influence of Buddhism and of one Mahāyāna sūtra during the first millenium A.D.

Seckel, Dietrich, trans. Ann E. Keep, *The Art of Buddhism.* New York: Crown Publishers, Inc., 1964. Buddhism as expressed in art forms throughout Asia; illustrated with color plates.

Welch, Holmes, *The Practice of Chinese Buddhism, 1900–1950.* Cambridge, Mass.: Harvard University Press, 1967. Based on interviews of Sangha refugees from the Communist-controlled mainland as well as documentary sources. Important study of a neglected subject; a good complement to the work of Prip-Møller. Excellent plates.

Thompson, Laurence G., *The Chinese Way in Religion.* Encino, Calif., and Belmont, Calif.: Dickenson Publishing Co., Inc., 1973. See Part Three: Buddhism.

Chang, Chen-chi, *The Practice of Zen.* London: Rider & Co., 1960. Authoritative exposition of yogic concentration in Chinese Buddhism; admirably succinct and lucid.

Luk, Charles (Lu K'uan-yü), *The Secrets of Chinese Meditation.* London: Rider & Co., 1964; papercover available. Deals clearly and well with techniques of various Buddhist and Taoist Schools.

TAOISM

Welch, Holmes, *The Parting of the Way.* London: Methuen & Co., Ltd.; Boston: Beacon Press, 1957; papercover available. See Part Three: The Taoist Movement. Good summary of what is presently known of the obscure history of religious Taoism; popular style.

Ware, James R., *Alchemy, Medicine, and Religion in the China of A.D. 320: The Nei P'ien of Ko Hung (Pao-p'u tzu).* Cambridge, Mass.: M.I.T. Press, 1966. Unannotated translation of important text.

Maspero, Henri, "Les Procédés de Nourir le Principe Vital dans la Religion Taoiste Ancienne," *Journal Asiatique,* Vol. 229, 1937. Still one of the basic studies.

Lu, K'uan-yü (Charles Luk), *Taoist Yoga. Alchemy and Immortality.* London: Rider & Co., 1970; papercover available. Translation of a modern text called The Secrets of Cultivating Essential Nature and Eternal Life.

Giles, Lionel, *A Gallery of Chinese Immortals.* London: John Murray, Ltd., 1948 (Wisdom of the East Series). Biographies of Taoist adepts who achieved immortality, taken from the popular literature.

Goullart, Peter, *The Monastery of Jade Mountain.* London: John Murray, Ltd., 1961. Rare autobiographical account by a sincere European Taoist; rather naive and sentimental, but contains much valuable material.

Saso, Michael R., *Taoism and the Rite of Cosmic Renewal.* Washington State University Press, 1972. Important as the first really "inside" account of the rituals, informed by the author's literary knowledge as well as his personal participation in rites on Taiwan.

Blofeld, John, *The Secret and Sublime; Taoist Mysteries and Magic.* London: Allen & Unwin, Ltd., 1973. Entertainingly written account of author's personal experiences, informed also by his knowledge of the literary sources. A basic work for understanding of Chinese Taoism at all of its levels.

Wilhelm, Richard, trans., *The Secret of the Golden Flower* (translated from German by Cary Baynes). New York: Harcourt Brace & World, Inc., 1931; revised ed., 1962; papercover, New York: Harcourt, Brace & World. Two basic texts of two Taoist sects. Extensive commentary by C. G. Jung, the value of which depends on one's opinion of Jung's ideas and Jung's understanding of Taoism (which he got mostly from Wilhelm).

Thompson, Laurence G., *The Chinese Way in Religion.* Encino, Calif., and Belmont, Calif.: Dickenson Publishing Co., Inc., 1973. See Part Two: Taoism.

Luk, Charles (Lu K'uan-yü), *The Secrets of Chinese Meditation.* London: Rider & Co., 1964; papercover available. Deals clearly and well with techniques of various Buddhist and Taoist schools

Rawson, Philip & Laszlo Legeza., *Tao, the Eastern Philosophy of Time and Change.* New York: Avon Books, 1973, papercover. Breaks new ground in showing pervasiveness of Taoist ideas in Chinese art: excellent Introduction, 196 plates.

LAYMEN'S RELIGION

Yang, C. K., *Religion in Chinese Society.* Berkeley and Los Angeles: University of California Press, 1961; papercover available. Best treatment of the subject.

Suzuki, T., and P. Carus, trans., *T'ai-Shang Kan-Ying P'ien.* Chicago: Open Court Publishing Co., 1906; reprinted in La Salle, Ill., 1950. Immensely popular tract, illustrative of the laymen's eclectic religion.

Suzuki, T. and P. Carus, trans., *Yin Wen Chih.* Chicago: Open Court Publishing Co., 1906; reprinted in La Salle, Ill., 1950. Another popular tract.

Plopper, Clifford H., *Chinese Religion Seen Through the Proverb.* Shanghai: China Press, 1926; reprinted in New York: Paragon, 1969. Thorough study of popular beliefs.

Eberhard, Wolfram, *Guilt and Sin in Traditional China.* Berkeley and Los Angeles: University of California Press, 1967. Analysis of materials in popular morality books and fiction; details on popular conceptions of hells. The author is an eminent sociologist-sinologist.

Thompson, Laurence G., *The Chinese Way in Religion.* Encino, Calif., and Belmont, Calif.: Dickenson Publishing Company, Inc., 1973. See Part Six: Popular Religion.

7.

The Festival Year

Cutting across social groups and voluntary institutions is the series of annual festivals observed by the entire nation. While many of these have in the course of time become drained of religious meaning (just as few of our present holidays are still holy-days), almost all of them derived from religious origins, and the majority continued to carry at least some religious significance.

The almanac told the people when the festival days were to occur each year, and the traditions of ages prescribed how they were to be celebrated. Still, there were any number of customs that varied from place to place. For this reason every gazetteer or local history had a section in which the festival calendar (*sui-shih*) of the particular locality was described in detail. Here we shall list only a few of the outstanding festivals that were universally observed, and some of the typical ways in which they were celebrated.

New Year

The concept of the new year is of course of great symbolic meaning among every people. In China it was by far the most important and elaborate of all the universal festivals. It actually began in the twelfth month when, about ten days before the end of the year, government offices (*yamen*) throughout the country closed down (literally, "sealed up their seals," *feng-yin*), not to reopen for business until about a month later. Then, on the twenty-third day of the twelfth month, in every home the God of the Cooking Stove (Tsao Chün or Tsao Wang) was sent off to heaven to report to the Jade Emperor (Yü Huang-ti), celestial ruler in the Taoist pantheon.

Tsao Chün, like the local earth god, has an importance in the lives of the people all out of proportion to the humbleness of his icons. He is ordinarily represented by a cheap and gaudy print that is pasted on the wall above the stove. This deity, whose worship dates back to the mid-second century B.C., is both guardian of the hearth and arbiter of longevity (in which role he is called Ssu-ming Fu-chün). His place behind the stove is strategically located for him to carry out the important function of keeping a daily record of the words and actions of the family, the sum of which it is his duty to report on his annual visit to heaven. A detail that writers are fond of mentioning is the custom of smearing his mouth with some sugary substance before transmuting him to the ethereal realm by burning, so that he will have only "sweet" things to tell.

As arbiter of the length of life that will be enjoyed by each family member, his function naturally seems a more serious one. How seriously this function is actually taken no doubt varies according to individual belief.

But it is in his role as deity of the kitchen range that he seems most significant. Because, whatever the "historical" background for this role, it is the stove that in fact stands for the unity of the Chinese family. As a number of recent studies have pointed out, "division of the stove" is both a symbolical and an actual event marking the splitting of the family, that is to say, the establishment of separate households by brothers after the death of their parents.

Tsao Chün returns to the home on new year's eve, when a new picture is pasted up over the stove. His is not the only symbol of renewal that goes up at this time: during the days preceding the new year every household puts up new "spring couplets" on either side of the gate and across the lintel. These are written on lucky red paper and consist of mottoes expressing the pious hope for blessings of all kinds to descend upon the household during the coming year. And then, on the leaves of the gates themselves are pasted bright pictures of fierce warriors who serve as guardians of the gate.

Rituals of new year's eve are for the family to observe within its own doors, which are sealed until the following morning. These rituals include the worship of Heaven and Earth, of the tutelary deities of the home, and of the ancestors. At the conclusion of these rites comes the family feast, which is attended by all members who can possibly be there—but by no outside guests. This ecumenical meal is another of the numerous practices by which family unity is reaffirmed. It is followed at midnight by an even more explicit ritual; all family members come forward in order of precedence to prostrate themselves and touch their foreheads to the floor (*k'o-t'ou* or kotow) to the family head and his wife.

The religious and familial rites having thus been performed, the first few days of the new year are devoted to pleasure and relaxation, and to paying courtesy calls upon one's seniors and superiors. All business is at a standstill, even now for as long as a week, and in past times for almost the entire first month.

Two religious ceremonies of importance that occurred during the first two weeks were the family and communal worship of Ts'ai Shen, God of Wealth, and the official performance of the rituals connected with the beginning of spring (*li ch'un*, first of the twenty-four "seasons" of the lunar calendar). In imperial times the emperor himself opened the agricultural year by ceremonially plowing a special field in the capital, this being emulated by the chief officials in every locality. Then came the religious procession headed by the "spring ox," an effigy whose color predicted the climatic conditions of the coming year (based upon information contained in the newly published almanac). Many other symbolic items and actions connected with this procession had to do with hopes for a prosperous agricultural year.

The first (new moon) and fifteenth (full moon) are naturally to an agricultural people the most noticeable markers of time in the lunar months, and it is not surprising that many ritual observances fall on one or both of these days. In the case of the new year, it is the first full moon that marks the end of the celebrations. This is the time for the lantern festival, originally no doubt of religious derivation, but in later centuries purely a holiday in which enjoyment of the beauty and ingenuity of the lanterns is the principal feature.

Third Month

The second of the great universal festivals falls 105 days after the winter solstice or, in recent times, on the third day of the third month. This is the fifth of the twenty-four lunar seasons, whose climatic character in north China gave it the name "clear and bright" (*ch'ing ming*). It is the most important of the three special occasions of the year for visiting the ancestral tombs, renovating them, and sacrificing to them. As such, it is part and parcel of the complex of continuing sacrifices to the manes which we have discussed in our chapter on the family. Here we should point out that in all these ancestral rites there are specific foci of interest. The vast majority of the ancestors inevitably pass into oblivion, or at least are only lumped together as the "common ancestors," while the attentions of the living center either upon their immediate, rememberable generations, or else upon the most important figures of the past—notably the founding ancestor of the lineage. It is to these tombs that the family goes on *ch'ing ming* and other days of remembrance, as it is from these tombs that "good *feng-shui*" may be sought.

The twenty-third day of the third month is the birthday of T'ien Hou, Imperial Consort of Heaven (see p. 60). Having been adopted into the official calendar of sacrifices, her birthday was marked everywhere in the empire. However, because she is primarily the protector of seafarers, and her cult developed south of the Yangtze river, the great popular festivals are found in the southeastern coastal provinces.

Fourth Month

The supposed birthday of the Buddha Śakyamuni occurs, according to Chinese calculations, on the eighth day of the fourth month. This is an occasion celebrated primarily by the Saṅgha. The principal rite is the "bathing of the Buddha," in which the Buddha image is laved with scented water. The temples will be filled, and there may be elaborate processions with the Buddha image borne in state by the monks.

Fifth Month

The third major universal celebration is that popularly known as the dragon boat festival, placed (in accordance with another Chinese propensity) on "double five," or the fifth day of the fifth month. The dragon boat races may very well represent the fighting of dragons in the skies and hence be related to abundance of rainfall, for which the dragon is responsible in Chinese lore. The festival is quite different in the north, which lacks the rivers and lakes on which such spectacles can be staged. The rationale of the boat races has long been understood as a reenactment of the search for the drowned poet Ch'ü Yüan, who committed suicide in ancient times because his honest counsel was spurned by his lord. The triangular-shaped dumplings traditionally eaten on this day are likewise supposed to stand for the food that the sorrowing people dropped into the water for Ch'ü Yüan's spirit.

But it would seem logical to seek the true origin of this important festival in the occurrence of the summer solstice, which falls at about the same time. This of course marks the highest expansion of the fructifying influence of *yang,* and the beginning of its gradual displacement by *yin,* an event of great significance in the Chinese world view. However, the double five festival is one of those that has declined into a purely secular occasion.

Seventh Month

This month sees the second of the major periods in the annual round that focuses upon the ancestors. During this entire month the gates of purgatory stand open and the souls of those who have no ancestral sacrifices—the hungry ghosts—are free to wander about in the invisible dimension that impinges upon the mortal world. Needless to say, during this month many special measures are taken by the living to placate these ghosts and avert harm. The fact that a whole month is involved in this problem of bereaved spirits is eloquent testimony to the profound importance of ancestral sacrifices.

But though this is as we know a native cult of the highest antiquity, it has, like most aspects of the mortuary rites, been largely taken over by Buddhism (and to a lesser extent Taoism). The hungry ghosts are identified with the Indian *preta.* The great services of sacrifice that take place in the middle of the month are called *yü-lan hui,* which is a Chinese rendering of the sanskrit term *Avalambana.* The officiants are monks who recite from the canonical Chinese text that tells of the filial piety of Mu-lien (Maudgalyāyana), who rescued his mother from the torture of the hell in which souls cannot eat. This he was able to do by the grace of the Buddha, who instructed him to make offerings on the fifteenth day of the seventh month to seven generations of ancestors. The ritual is called "ferrying across [to the other shore of salvation] all [souls in limbo or purgatory]" (*p'u tu*), a Buddhist term. The populace participates in the extensive ceremonies, particularly through their generous offerings.

Eighth Month

No festival is more common, throughout the world, than the celebration of the autumn harvest. In China this has been transformed into a celebration of the beauty of the harvest moon, at its most perfect on the fifteenth night of the eighth month. Although its religious element long ago faded, this festival is one of the most popular in the year. The traditional gift is circular "moon cakes," and the people feast out of doors enjoying the glorious moon until late at night.

Ninth Month

If the moon festival celebrates the most conspicuous *yin* force in the heavens, the "double *yang*" (*ch'ung yang*) is, in name at least, the polar opposite. Alas for our hope to find some significant symbolism; the name simply reflects the fact that the unbroken lines in the diagrams of the *Yi Ching* are technically called nines, and this festival falls on the ninth day of the ninth month. No religious element seems to remain in what is a minor event in the festival calendar, marked only by picnics (preferably in the hills) and kite flying.

Tenth Month

On the first day of the tenth month the ancestors are especially remembered for the third time, as the family pays ritual visits to their tombs. In addition to the usual sending of mock paper money, the dead are provided with paper effigies of warm clothes for the winter, and any other articles it is thought they might want. The ritual is called "sending cold weather clothes" (*sung han yi*).

Twelfth Month

Various observances during the twelfth month are, as we have seen, by way of being a prelude to the great festival of the new year. The winter solstice is marked by sacrifices as the day on which the potency of *yin* reaches its extreme, to be gradually replaced by the life-nurturing power of *yang*. On the eighth day of the month it is the custom to serve friends with a special gruel made of many ingredients, which is also presented as an offering to the Buddha. This is called *la-pa chou,* and the entire month is sometimes designated by the first word of the term. (*La* was the name of a sacrifice connected with the winter solstice in antiquity; *pa* means the eighth [day]; and *chou* means gruel.) Then come the "sealing up of the seals" and the ritual of sending Tsao Chün to heaven, and the old year gives way again to the new.

All the festivals are timed in accordance with the lunar, agricultural calendar, and even official adoption of the solar calendar decades ago and its everyday use has not affected the universal usage of the old calendar in governing celebration of the festival year; it is this calendar that is still printed in the almanac.

SELECTED READINGS

Hodous, Lewis, *Folkways in China.* London: Arthur Probsthain, 1929. The round of the festival year, and some major deities, with special reference to the Foochow area.

Burkhardt, V. R., *Chinese Creeds and Customs.* Hong Kong: South China Morning Post, Ltd., 1953–58, 3 vols. See particularly Vol. 1 for the festival calendar.

Wong, C. S., *A Cycle of Chinese Festivities.* Singapore: Malaysia Publishing House, Ltd., 1967. The festivals as celebrated in Malaysia by overseas Chinese, together with researches in literary sources.

Bredon, Juliet, and Igor Mitrophanow, *The Moon Year.* Shanghai: Kelly & Walsh, Ltd., 1927; reprinted New York: Paragon, 1966. Many details about religious and other customs, written around the framework of the festival calendar. Common Chinese beliefs, presented in an interesting popular style.

8.

Disruption of the Tradition

The Chinese civilization was, until the mid-nineteenth century, essentially an original, self-contained system. It was a civilization which historically had been superior to its neighbors, and which had indeed been the source of the high cultures of all East Asia.

This Chinese civilization was immensely long-lived, rich, and satisfying to the Chinese. It had the scope and the local variations of a grand continental scale, but the pervading unity of a great traditional culture. The only imported influence of significance in this civilization was Buddhism—which in its turn was profoundly modified in its accommodation to Chinese ways. The Chinese view of nature and man, and the Chinese social practices (*li*) did not change in any great measure since ancient times. That is why in this book we have been able to describe Chinese religion without specifying the historical tense.

During the past century and before, however, China entered a new era. Its civilization was no longer self-contained, evidently superior, or even satisfying to the Chinese people. By the rude insistence of the aggressive Western powers during the nineteenth century, and by the even more irresistible impact of modern science and technology and all that these bring in their train, China was forced into an unprecedented situation. Part of the problem was the necessity to modernize without the gradual evolutionary process which brought Europe from medieval to modern conditions. Even more serious was the trauma resulting from the realization that the whole position of China had altered so that, far from being the center of human culture, she was now, in fact, a backward culture in a modern world.

During the first half of the twentieth century the most salient characteristic of China was turbulent change—political upheaval, rampant militarism, an economy struggling to emerge from medieval limitations, a dangerously burgeoning population, a succession of tremendous natural disasters resulting in famines and plagues of unimaginable dimensions, a society torn between tradition and modernization. The political and military chaos that had always accompanied the "change of the Mandate" when one dynasty replaced another was exacerbated to unprecedented degrees by the involvement of Western and Japanese imperialistic pressures and interventions, culminating in the full-scale invasion and occupation of much of China by Japanese armies from 1937 to 1945.

There was not one but several revolutions in this era. The revolution of 1911, although militarily a minor incident, accomplished a major change: the overthrow of the imperial system that had existed for two thousand years. The victory of the Nationalists in 1927 brought a first measure of unity to a nation that had since 1912 been torn by sectional strife and warlord rivalries. The revolution of 1949 brought to a successful conclusion the epic, thirty-year struggle by the Communists to impose a socialist system on China. Thus, the revolutions of the twentieth century were fundamentally different from revolutions of China's past. Those had changed the dynasty but preserved the system: new actors simply replaced the old, and tradition was restored. The twentieth century revolutions changed the actors, but much more importantly, they attacked the whole traditional system.

Although not a revolution in the political sense, another upheaval of the most profound consequence should be mentioned here. That is the New Culture Movement, or Renaissance, which began with an attack on the old literature and education in 1917, erupted into a nationwide student protest in May 1919, and developed on many fronts throughout the following decade. In its original form the attack was against the persistence of the use of a "dead language"—classical Chinese—in a world in which young Chinese desperately needed to think (and hence to write) in modern ways; it was also against the monopolization of education by the few who could afford the time and effort required to master the classical language in a day when republican and democratic movements called for universal literacy.

The great student demonstrations, which erupted on 4 May 1919 in protest against the "sellout" of China's national interests at the Paris Peace Conference, were significant as the first unified expression of the determination of the younger generation to bring to a halt the almost century-long series of humiliations inflicted upon China by the Powers. The New Culture Movement was driven by this strong determination, although there was no unanimity as to the best way in which to proceed. But although on the surface the destiny of China seemed to be in the hands of those representing only ignorance and reaction—the warlords—the real wave of the future moving powerfully underneath was the young intellectuals (the term in China meant anyone with so much as an elementary school education) who were going through an agonizing struggle to find China's new Way. What they demanded was national union, restoration of sovereignty, modern education, a new society purged of all the traditional evils, and in fact, a new China that would take its rightful place as a great nation in the world of the twentieth century. Thousands of these students went abroad to Europe and the United States (whereas a couple of decades or so earlier most went to Japan) and brought back with them the new ideas gained from their experiences in foreign lands. As would be expected, these ideas were varied and often self-contradictory as well as antitraditional. Out of a thousand debates and literary battles lines were formed; groups advocating one or another position in regard to science, education, politics, religion, literature and art, combined and dissolved, attacked and were attacked. In the decade following the May Fourth Movement such struggles may have seemed almost fruitless, but they were part of the great effort to overthrow the weight of tradition and found a modern China.

As a part of this traditional system religion could not, of course, escape this effort. In the discussion that follows we shall analyze some of the ways in which religion has been subjected to powerful forces for change during recent decades.

The World View. The rise of scientific secularism in the West occurred coincidentally with the strongest impact of Western political and economic power on China, at the end of the 19th and during the early 20th centuries. In this period the Chinese were subjected both to a strong barrage of Christian propaganda and to its counterinfluence, atheistic or at least scientific materialism. By the nineteen-twenties and thirties this warfare of Western ideas had become the most important factor in the intellectual world of China, where it was of course complicated by the existence of native traditions opposed to both foreign creeds. Every shade of opinion, from the most conservative to the most radical, was represented. Slowly but surely the conservative gave way as the weight of the most able intellectuals shifted to the side of "science"—whether physical or economic (Marxist).

Still, it cannot be said that the world view of the Chinese as a whole was much affected by the conquests of Western science and philosophy. This particular battle was fought out among a tiny handful of intellectuals, and hardly touched the thinking of the vast majority of the people. The small number of Buddhist thinkers had no reason to feel any erosion of their basic premises. The higher philosophy of Buddhism, far from being antagonistic to the spirit or methods of science, is readily adaptive to the new ways, regarding as it does all knowledge of the phenomenal world as being on the level of relative truth. No more sophisticated or final theory of Reality is ever likely to be devised by the mind of man than the "non-theory" of *śūnyatā*. The native cosmology based on *tao, yin* and *yang,* the five elemental operative qualities, and all their associated concepts were by no means swept away. Perhaps they will never be swept away, since Western science and philosophy can hardly offer more satisfactory alternatives. Even on the formal philosophical level the victory of Western concepts might ultimately prove ephemeral, since there was apparently a surprising vitality in neo-Confucian thought.

Family Religion. The strong family system of the Chinese was under great stress during the period. As industrialization progressed the cities drew increasing numbers of workers from the rural environs, and urban conditions of life tended to break down family cohesion. With economic independence derived from factory wage-earning came a certain amount of freedom of choice for the individual and the weakening of the authority of family elders. Modern education furthered this process, both because many students lived away from their homes, and because their books were strongly influenced by Western individualistic thought. Even the chaotic conditions brought about by political instability and continual fighting contributed to the same result, as millions of persons became homeless or were pressed into military service.

The result of these and many other factors was the erosion of parental control, the weakening of lineage loyalties, and a sense of isolation and alienation among individuals. When the Communist regime came to power, it was able to capture the allegiance of millions of persons who welcomed a new focus for their loyalties—and of course that regime has given its most determined efforts to substituting loyalty to the Party and State for loyalty to the family. It would be overstating the success of these efforts to claim that the traditional family has already succumbed, but there is no doubt that there is a significant new orientation towards the welfare of "the people" as against the benefits to one's family group.

The implications of these developments for the ancestral cult are obvious. If that cult was in essence the symbolical cement holding together a structure of families and lineage, then the disintegration of family and lineage is prima facie evidence of the weakening of the ancestral cult. If our view is correct—that this family cult has been the basic, universal religion of the Chinese—then it is further apparent that its disruption implies the most serious consequences for Chinese civilization. Indeed it is not difficult to find many examples of profound changes that have already occurred in specific places where the process of dissolution is far advanced.

Community Religion. Community religion, as we have described it, is equally caught up in a vortex of change. Formerly isolated communities are being exposed to many outside influences. Their exclusiveness and unity are breaking down. Their inhabitants travel to the cities, work in factories, serve in the army. Roads and railways bring the world closer. Education arrives, and the efficacy of the gods is called into question. The rudiments of modern schooling spread scientific explanations of cause and effect, and the animistic beliefs lose their rationale. This process has been going on for more than a century, and long before the Communist government pushed its campaigns against superstitions, temples throughout the country had been allowed to fall into disuse, or had been converted to secular uses. Such a trend seems irreversible.

State Religion. Upon the collapse of the imperial polity in 1911 the whole structure of the state religion disappeared. Subsequent governments were generally indifferent, if not hostile, to religion. The Nationalist regime in the early nineteenthirties sponsored a revival of the ancient Confucian ethic as a matter of official policy. This included annual observance of the ritual in the *wen miao* on the birthday of the Sage, the celebration being named Teachers' Day, however. The position of the Communist regime is naturally in accord with the dictum of Marx, that "religion is the opiate of the people." Unless one feels that the annual rituals in T'ien-an Men Square in Peking on May Day, or the cult of Chairman Mao as exemplified especially in the Great Proletarian Cultural Revolution are religious in nature, the State has no religion.*

*That this cult, and Communism as a whole system in its Chinese form, are themselves truly religious, has been asserted by many writers.

One quasi-religious feature under both regimes is the daily ritual of bowing to the portraits of the Leaders which hang in every classroom and office. The Nationalist Leader is Sun Yat-sen, while that of the Communists is of course Mao Tse-tung. One might choose to think of this as a continuation of the tradition of memorial halls to great men rather than a Chinese form of the "pledge of allegiance." Sun Yat-sen has long since acquired all the legendary essentials of the Founding Father, while to a still living Mao Tse-tung have been attributed even more potent mythic qualities as a semidivinity. "Kingship" still requires the aura of religious charisma.

Institutionalized Religion. As the more conspicuous of the institutionalized religions, Buddhism is naturally of special interest when we are considering the travails of religion in the twentieth century. Despite a small flurry of activity during the first four decades of the century which sometimes led observers to conclude that they were witnessing a revitalization of Chinese Buddhism, it has become apparent from more careful study[1] that this was an illusion. Much of this activity was superficial, an attempt to "modernize" the religion in competition with Christianity, a series of social, political, and economic moves that were more a desperate defense against the forces inimical to Buddhism than a manifestation of recreative vitality.

The forces referred to are the same ones we have already mentioned, including scientific secularism, Christian propaganda, complex processes of industrialization and modernization, and disruption of the traditional family and social systems. If young Chinese intellectuals turned to any religion it was apt to be Christianity, which was somehow associated with the power and progress of advanced Western nations (despite the incongruity of that association within Western civilization itself). Buddhism, a religion advocating withdrawal from the world rather than struggle within it, was completely unrelated to the urgent needs of China as these young people saw it. The more Buddhist leaders tried to bring their religion and its institutions into some sort of relevance to the situation, the farther they took these from their true character. *Irrelevance* to social and political movements was inherent in Chinese Buddhism; a "social gospel" was incongruous. The Chinese ideal of the monk or nun was precisely the recluse devoted to holy ritual and yogic meditation.

Under Nationalist control the State did not persecute Buddhism, but it was not interested either in nurturing it. As for the Communists, Buddhism fell into the same category as all other religion—an instrument of a "feudal" exploitation of the masses that would not be tolerated. Communist policy towards religious institutions has been to utilize them when they could be made to serve the interests of the Party line, and otherwise to encourage their demise. Because there was some small value in international relations with the so-called Buddhist countries of Southeast Asia for the Chinese to seem to patronize the religion, this game was played. A malleable group of monks was organized into the Chinese Buddhist Association (continuing a name from Republican times) which could "represent"

Chinese Buddhism to the outside world, and which attempted mollification of international Buddhist outrage at such harsh anti-Buddhist actions as the persecutions in Tibet. A few of the well-known temples and monasteries were maintained as showcases for Buddhist visitors, and a few books and magazines were published for external consumption. All of this could not disguise the fact that Buddhism had ceased to play an institutional role in Communist Chinese society.

During the excesses of the Great Proletarian Revolution in the late nineteen-sixties it seemed that practically every monastery in China had shut down. Without the economic basis of land rentals the monasteries could hardly survive in any case. And in the new society of the People's Republic, it is difficult indeed to justify the monastic life, when all activities must be measured against the obligation of "service to the masses."

As for institutionalized Taoism, it has received very little attention from scholars in this century. One can only say that its fate has in general paralleled that of Buddhism. It had far fewer monastic centers than Buddhism, but on the other hand it had a much more intimate association with the folk religion: many of its professional religious served as priests and mediums and exorcists. Therefore its survival power may be greater than that of the Buddhist saṅgha.

This close association with folk religion is not an unmixed advantage, however; it brings Taoism under the same rubric as "superstitions" and causes it to be an object of contempt of the intelligentsia and an object of persecution by the government. The Communist regime has been even more outspokenly opposed to superstitions than are the Nationalists: while article 88 of the constitution of 1954 guarantees "freedom of religious belief,"[2] such freedom explicitly does not extend to "superstitions."

The single most important symbol of institutionalized Taoism was the "heavenly master" Chang (Chang *t'ien-shih*) of the southern school (see p. 102). The incumbent, sixty-third in the line, fled when Communist forces arrived, and his great ancestral estates in Kiangsi province were confiscated. Thus was eliminated the only nationally important center for certification or ordination of Taoist priests.

Institutionalized Taoism must be considered by the Communist government rather on a different basis from Buddhism. That is to say, it is actually a potential threat to the State because of its historical involvement with secret societies and political insurrection. This again is a concomitant of its close connections with the religion of the folk.

Confucius and the Great Tradition. The most important casualty of these revolutionary times is Confucius: by this is meant the whole religious, ethical, educational, literary, and political backbone of the traditional Chinese civilization based upon the Confucian Canon. The damage done to the Chinese Great Tradition by the collapse of Confucian authority is even more serious than the profound changes wrought in Western society by the attacks of scientific secularism on traditional religion.

The outward signal of the death of Confucian authority was the abolishment in 1905 of the imperial examinations with their degrees, thus doing away with the very raison d'etre of traditional education. Increasingly, as Western influences penetrated the minds of China's intellectuals, Confucius came to stand for an anachronistic system of values that was a veritable millstone about the neck of progress. With the victory of modern education—that is, textbooks written in the colloquial language rather than the language of the Classics—in the early nineteen-twenties, study of the Confucian Canon became not only irrelevant to the attainment of status in the modern society, but an antiquarian pursuit of interest only to the limited number willing to spend the considerable effort required to comprehend the ancient texts.

It is true that when the Nationalist government in the early nineteen-thirties felt the need to counter the ideological program of the Communists, they turned to the Confucian Canon as the only viable source of an authentic native tradition. But their efforts to inspire youth through required courses on Confucian texts in the middle schools and universities cannot be said to have been successful.

Thus, if one takes the most extreme view, one concludes that Confucian civilization is really dead, and that some entirely new national character must replace the old tradition. This is of course the thesis of the leadership on the mainland. The apparently erratic policies of Mao Tse-tung have as their unvarying goal the extirpation of "feudal" remnants in China's society (most of which are "Confucian"), the creation of a new people whose ideals are those of revolutionary socialism, not Confucianism, and of course ultimately the utopia of a true communistic society. In Taiwan, on the other hand, there is an outspoken challenge to this effort, as the Nationalist government continues—perhaps in a somewhat more effective manner than before—to assert the values of traditional Confucian civilization as the true Chinese culture, while at the same time pursuing completely modern goals in the social and economic spheres.

Taiwan and Overseas. In considering the religious situation of the second half of this century one must thus look not only at the mainland, but also at the island province of Taiwan and the many millions of Chinese residing overseas (mostly in Hong Kong and Southeast Asia). While there is great variety in the religious picture from place to place, in general it may be accurate to say that traditional religion is more flourishing among Chinese outside than inside the mainland. Certainly in the case of Taiwan one would need to modify many of the generalities offered above. There one finds a strong family (although not necessarily a strong lineage) system operative. There the folk religion is flourishing. There Buddhism is enjoying a genuine renaissance, both as a popular religion and as a monastic vocation.* Christianity, whose missionaries still operate in force on the island, has made a strong impression. Temple building in Taiwan redoubled as if in direct challenge to the iconoclasm of the Cultural Revolution on the mainland,

*There seem never to have been any Taoist monasteries in Taiwan. There are, however, many professional religious who function at the folk religion level.

while all the government's stern injunctions against "waste" have failed to dampen the exuberant extravagance of the Taiwanese religious festivals (*pai-pai*).

We opened our discussion with the statement that we wished to view Chinese religion as primarily an expression of the Chinese culture. It is an obvious concomitant of that view that as the culture changes so must the religion. The future of religion in China is thus integrally bound up with the question of cultural change; therefore, the basic question is the outcome of the gigantic experiment that has been taking place on the mainland of China since 1949. It seems self-evident that it is as much a misjudgment to find that Communist China is something entirely novel as that it is merely a continuation of the old in a new guise. Yet long before the Communists established their control China had changed and was changing drastically, as our earlier remarks have indicated. It seems most unlikely that we have yet come to a point of stability in this process, and indeed it is the most basic premise of Chairman Mao and his followers that revolution must continue for a long time to come if Communist goals are to be achieved. Entirely aside from this ideologically required revolution is the fact that the attainment of "modernity" in a society in itself assures a condition that seems part and parcel of that modernity: ceaseless, restless change.

It may be that looked at from a certain point of view, religion in a dramatic and totally unexpected form manifested itself throughout the Chinese society of the first quarter-century under Communist rule. Thus, while the observer sees on the one hand the decline or repression of the traditional modes, on the other he cannot help but be impressed by a remarkable "change of heart" throughout the Chinese society. Concern for others and service to the people as the highest goals cannot be shrugged away as propaganda. Their leaders have succeeded in imbuing the populace as a whole with these ideals, and the fervor with which they have been adopted is unmistakable. In the striking words of one foreign authority: "If religion is considered as more than an institution—if it is seen, say, as the belief in and practice of love at every social level—then China must be one of the world's most successful religions."[3] It is this spirit, in fact, that Mao Tse-tung knows it will be necessary, and dreams it will be possible, to maintain and eventually to become the indestructible root of the Chinese society in ages to come.

Any attempt to predict the forms Chinese religion will take in the future, especially in view of this totally new development, would obviously be foolish. What we can assert is the necessity of understanding the traditional forms in our effort to understand the whole culture of the past, and in the broader task of understanding religious man in the universal framework. And we can be sure, as we reflect on history, that even the seemingly most drastic changes or suppressions of forms do not guarantee the outcome: religious forms, like certain plants, can remain dormant for a very long time, only to spring up again when the environment becomes favorable.

SELECTED READINGS

Hughes, E. R., *The Invasion of China by the Western World*. London: A. & C. Black, 1937; New York: Macmillan Co., 1938. Still the best survey of nonpolitical aspects.

Franke, Wolfgang, *A Century of Chinese Revolution, 1851–1949*. New York: Harper Torchbooks, 1970 (papercover). Amid a plethora of books on nineteenth and twentieth century political history, this is a good, concise summary.

Brière, O., trans. L. G. Thompson, *Fifty Years of Chinese Philosophy, 1898–1950*. London: George Allen & Unwin, Ltd., 1956; papercover, New York: Frederick A. Praeger, Inc., 1965. Brief but comprehensive, emphasizing the tensions between traditional Chinese and imported Western views.

Chan, Wing-tsit, *Religious Trends in Modern China*. New York: Columbia University Press, 1953. Authoritative survey based on a wide range of literary sources.

Yang, C. K., *Religion in Chinese Society*. Berkeley and Los Angeles: University of California Press, 1961; papercover available. See chapters 13 and 14.

Bush, Richard C., Jr., *Religion in Communist China*. Nashville and New York: Abingdon Press, 1970. Thorough, careful, and objective study based on Communist sources; lucidly written.

MacInnis, Donald E., *Religious Policy and Practice in Communist China*. New York: MacMillan Co.; London: Collier-MacMillan Ltd., 1972; papercover available. Excellent documentary history, which complements the work of Bush.

Thompson, Laurence G., *The Chinese Way in Religion*. Encino, Calif., and Belmont, Calif.: Dickenson Publishing Co., Inc., 1973. See Postscript: Religion under Communism.

Welch, Holmes, *The Buddhist Revival in China*. Cambridge, Mass.: Harvard University Press, 1968. Twentieth century prior to Communist takeover. Section of photographs by Henri Cartier-Bresson. Careful, objective study.

Welch, Holmes, *Buddhism under Mao*. Cambridge, Mass.: Harvard University Press, 1972. Thorough study by the leading authority. Many plates.

Appendix: The Confucian Canon

The Confucian Canon occupies a position in Chinese culture comparable to that occupied in the West by the Bible plus the major works of Greek and Roman literature. From the mid-second century B.C. to the twentieth century, the Canon formed the minds of all educated Chinese, providing the content of the educational curriculum and the guiding principles of philosophy, statecraft, personal and social ethics, and religion. Those who mastered these works became the elite, the literati, eligible by virtue of this learning to be appointed as officials in the imperial government.

The two institutionalized religions, Buddhism and Taoism, also had their canons. However, these were studied for the most part by the professional religious, their technical language rendering them almost unintelligible to nonspecialists. Their influence in Chinese culture cannot be compared in scope or profundity with that of the Confucian Canon.

The contents of this Confucian "Bible" were not determined once and for all at a certain time. The core works which were always included consisted of the *Shu, Shih, Yi, Ch'un-Ch'iu,* and *Li.* A Canon of Music is said already to have been lost by Han times. From the early Han dynasty on, the *Lun-Yü, Meng Tzu, Hsiao Ching,* and *Erh Ya* were also singled out for special study and may be said to have had quasi-canonical status.

In the Han period there was considerable controversy over the establishment of correct texts. In 124 B.C. an imperial university was founded in the capital for the teaching of the Confucian scriptures—an institution whose importance may be judged from its enrollment, which is said to have reached some 30,000 students. The texts were engraved on stone in A.D. 175 and again between A.D. 240 and 248. In T'ang times the Canon comprised thirteen works, while in the Sung dynasty the Neo-Confucian philosophers edited a revised version divided into the Five *Ching* (scriptures) and the Four Books. The former included the *Shu, Shih, Yi, Ch'un-ch'iu* with three commentaries, and *Li Chi,* while the latter comprised *Lun-Yü, Chung-Yung, Ta-Hsüeh,* and *Meng Tzu.* This Sung version, equipped with the commentaries of Chu Hsi (1130–1200)—who has aptly been dubbed the Thomas Aquinas of Confucianism—remained the orthodox Canon until the twentieth century.

1.SHU CHING: CANON OF HISTORICAL DOCUMENTS (OR BOOK OF HISTORY)

Documents purporting to record words and deeds of ancient rulers from the legendary Yao to the early Chou (about 1000 B.C.). Although some of these documents were already recognized as forgeries in Han times, the entire text was considered by most Chinese as scripture.

B. Karlgren, *The Book of Documents* (Stockholm, 1950); J. Legge, *The Shoo King* (Oxford 1865).

2. SHIH CHING: CANON OF POEMS (OR BOOK OF ODES; OR BOOK OF SONGS)

Anthology of songs from the feudal states of early Chou; the first and one of the greatest works of Chinese literature *per se.*

J. Legge, *The She King* (Oxford, 1871 and 1895); A. Waley, *The Book of Songs* (London 1937); B. Karlgren, *The Book of Odes* (Stockholm 1950); E. Pound, *The Confucian Odes* (Harvard 1954). See also M. Granet, *Festivals and Songs of Ancient China* (New York 1932).

3. YI (OR I) CHING: CANON OF CHANGES
See chapter 2 for discussion.

J. Legge, *The Yi King* (Oxford 1899, 2nd ed.); R. Wilhelm (English translation from German by Cary Baynes), *The I Ching, or Book of Changes* (New York 1950); J. Blofeld, *The Book of Change* (London 1965). See also H. Wilhelm, *Change: Eight Lectures on the I Ching* (New York 1960).

4. CH'UN-CH'IU: SPRING AND AUTUMN

Accompanied by three commentaries (*chuan*) named for their supposed authors: *Kung-yang Chuan, Ku-liang Chuan,* and *Tso Chuan.* Chronicle of the feudal state of Lu for the years 722–484 B.C. Attributed to Confucius himself. To make it fully intelligible the commentaries were added, that of Tso being by far the most detailed.

J. Legge, *The Ch'un Ts'ew with the Tso Chuen* (Oxford 1872).

5. LI CHING: CANON OF RITUAL AND PROTOCOL

This title covers three works on *li: Chou Li: Rituals of Chou; Yi (or I) Li: Ceremonial and Ritual;* and *Li Chi: Records of Ritual and Protocol.* The latter two have been cited several times in this book (see Chapter 3). These texts of the Confucian school were compiled in the early Han (second century B.C.), but undoubtedly their contents are much older. *Li Chi* is not only the fullest in detail, but is also rich in materials of a philosophical nature. (There is in addition a work of a similar nature, *Ta Tai Li Chi: Records of Ritual and Protocol Compiled by Tai Senior,* which is of quasi-canonical status.)

J. Legge, *The Li Ki* (Oxford 1885). J. Steele, *The I Li* (London 1917). E. Biot, *Le Tcheou-li ou Rites des Tcheou* (Paris 1851) (no English translation of *Chou Li* available).

6. LUN YÜ: ANALECTS
Compilation by later generation of followers; notes recording words and actions of Confucius and his disciples. Fragmentary and often perplexing, it is nevertheless the most nearly contemporary document, much of it having the ring of verbatim quotation of the Master's dicta.

Among many translations see J. Legge, *Confucian Analects* (Oxford 1892, 2nd ed.); A. Waley, *The Analects of Confucius* (London 1938).

7. CHUNG YUNG: DOCTRINE OF THE MEAN
A small work, originally a chapter in *Li Chi,* singled out for special attention by Chu Hsi as one of the Four Books. Traditionally ascribed to Tzu Ssu, grandson of Confucius, it deals with the personal and political implications of human nature and self-cultivation.

J. Legge, *The Doctrine of the Mean* (Oxford 1892, 2nd ed.); E. R. Hughes, *The Great Learning and The Mean-in-Action* (New York 1943); Ku, Hung-ming, *The Conduct of Life* (included in Lin, Yutang, editor, *The Wisdom of China and India,* New York 1942).

8.TA HSÜEH: THE GREAT LEARNING
Like the preceding, a short chapter extracted from *Li Chi* by Chu Hsi and included as one of the Four Books. Dates perhaps to around the time of Mencius, a century after the death of Confucius (that is, fourth century B.C.). Its theme is the ordering of society through self-cultivation of the individual.

J. Legge, *The Great Learning* (Oxford 1892, 2nd ed.); E. R. Hughes, *op. cit.*

9. MENG TZU: MENCIUS
The Philosopher Meng has aptly been called "the St. Paul to Confucius." The book bearing his name contains lengthy conversations which give us a good understanding of his thought. It may have been compiled under his personal supervision; in any case, it is a production dating from his own time (390–305 B.C.).

J. Legge, *The Works of Mencius* (Oxford 1892, 2nd ed.); D. C. Lau, *Mencius* (Middlesex, England: Penguin Books, 1970).

10. HSIAO CHING: CANON OF FILIALITY
A small work of unknown date and authorship, probably compiled prior to Han (say, third century B.C.), reflecting the great emphasis placed upon the cardinal virtue of filiality by the Confucian school.

J. Legge, *The Hsiao King* (Oxford 1899, 2nd ed.); Sister Mary Makra, *The Hsiao Ching* (St. John's University 1961).

11. ERH YA

The first Chinese dictionary, a lexicon compiled at least as early as the Han dynasty. No translation available.

Notes

All translations not otherwise credited are the author's own. The order of Chinese names is surname first, followed by given name. The Latinized versions of two names, Confucius and Mencius, have become accepted from long usage.

Preface

1. Herbert A. Giles, trans., *Strange Stories from A Chinese Studio* (4th rev. ed.) (Shanghai: Kelly & Walsh, 1926), Appendix I, p. 478.
2. Joseph Edkins, *Chinese Buddhism* (1st ed.) (London: Kegan Paul, Trench, Trubner & Co., n.d.; preface dated 1879), pp. 274 f.
3. Arthur F. Wright, *Buddhism in Chinese History* (Stanford, Calif.: Stanford University Press, 1959), p. 134, gives as "a generous estimate . . . one-thousandth of one per cent."

Chapter 1

1. Joseph Needham has thoroughly developed this theme. See his *Science and Civilization in China* (Cambridge, England: Cambridge University Press, 1956), Vol. II, Chap. 18, "Human Law and the Laws of Nature in China and the West."
2. *Yi Ching,* "Hsi Tz'u" II.
3. "Hung Fan" is generally regarded as a late Chou addition.
4. *Chung Yung,* XIII, 1.
5. Ku, Hung-ming, trans., *The Conduct of Life* (Taipei: privately published, 1956), p. 25.
6. *Lun Yü (Analects),* IV, 15.1, 2.
7. Wing-tsit Chan, trans., *The Way of Lao Tzu* (Indianapolis, Ind.: The Bobbs-Merrill Company, Inc., 1963), p. 97.
8. *Shu Ching,* "Hung Fan," in *The Book of Documents,* B. Karlgren, trans., *Bulletin of the Museum of Far Eastern Antiquities* (Stockholm, No. 22, 1950), pp. 34–35.
9. *Ibid.,* "Kin t'eng," p. 36.
10. Fung, Yu-lan, trans., *Chuang Tzu* (Shanghai: Commercial Press, 1933), Chap. 6, pp. 122 f.
11. *Meng Tzu (Mencius)* IIIA. 4.8
12. *Li Chi,* "Li Yün."
13. *Analects* XII,19.

Chapter 2

1. In order to correct this system to accord with the actual number of days in a solar year, the Chinese had already, as far back as the testimony of the oracle bones (described in Chapter 3) takes us, devised the Metonic Cycle, which provided for seven intercalary

months within every nineteen years. See Tung, Tso-pin, "The Chinese and the World's Ancient Calendars," *A Symposium on the World Calendar* (Taipei, Taiwan: Chinese Association for the United Nations, 1951). Fullest treatment of Chinese astronomical achievements is given by Needham, *op.cit.,* Vol. III.

2. John Lossing Buck, *Land Utilization in China* (Shanghai: Commercial Press, 1937), p. 392.

3. John Shryock has called attention, however, to one significant difference between the animistic spirits in general and those of the ancestors. It was not uncommon for men to coerce their deities, as when a magistrate would order the image of the god exposed to the broiling sun in case the god had failed to respond to prayers for rain. But no matter what the circumstances, "no Chinese would think of insulting or reproving his ancestors." See *The Origin and Development of the State Cult of Confucius* (New York and London: Century, 1932), p. 91, note 20.

4. For much of the material in the preceding two paragraphs we are indebted to the illuminating discussion in Needham, *op.cit.,* Vol II, 13(g).

5. E. J. Eitel, *Fêng-Shui: Principles of the Natural Science of the Chinese* (Hong Kong and London: Trubner, 1873), pp. 22 f.

6. *Ibid.,* pp. 48 ff.

7. *Ibid.,* p. 54.

8. For the compass used in *feng-shui* (and its connection with the history of the navigational compass), see Needham, *op. cit.,* Vol. IV, 26(i).

9. There were ten "heavenly stems" and twelve "earthly branches," and they were combined in order in the following manner: IA, IIB, IIIC, and so forth. A complete cycle thus produced sixty combinations. This system, found on oracle bones of the late Shang dynasty, is still used today to number the years, much as we have used cycles of one hundred years.

10. One cannot dismiss the purely aesthetic aspects of *feng-shui.* Aesthetic considerations unquestionably constituted an important component of the theory as it developed, and the vitality of the whole pseudo-science was no doubt due in no small measure to this fact.

11. The foregoing is a general characterization of *feng-shui* in its modern form. The origins of this pseudo-science may be traced back to late Chou times, but it seems that it began to become established as a system during the post-Han centuries (around A.D. 300).

12. Alan J. A. Elliott, *Chinese Spirit Medium Cults in Singapore* (London: The London School of Economics and Political Science, Department of Anthropology, 1955), p. 161.

13. Condensed from V. R. Burkhardt, *Chinese Creeds and Customs* (Hong Kong: South China Morning Post, Limited, 1953–58), Vol. II, pp. 144–148.

14. The use of fetishes must be as ancient as magical religion itself, but documentation goes back only to the first century A.D. (Wang Ch'ung, *Critical Essays, Lun Heng,* "Lan-Shih"). See Alfred Forke, *Lun-Hêng* (London: Luzac, 1907–11), Vol. II, pp. 38 f.

15. Burkhardt, *op. cit.,* Vol. II, pp. 142 f. Asterisks supplied.

16. Condensed from Peter Goullart, *The Monastery of Jade Mountain* (London: John Murray (Publishers), Ltd., 1961), pp. 86–89.

Chapter 3

1. Tung, Tso-in, *An Interpretation of the Ancient Chinese Civilization* (Taipei, Taiwan: Chinese Association for the United Nations, 1952), p. 19.

2. *Ibid.,* p. 19. Quotation from *Chung Yung* XIX.

3. *Ibid.,* p. 21.

4. This is again an oversimplification. In reality, because the ancestral cult is a reflection of the specific history, structure, and functioning of a particular community, it is expressed in widely varying ways. See especially Emily M. Ahern. *The Cult of the Dead in a Chinese Village* (Stanford: Stanford University Press, 1973), Conclusion, pp. 245–266.

5. For convincing evidence of this latter assertion, one may consult the detailed discussion of funeral rites in J. J. M. de Groot, *The Religious System of China* (Leiden, Netherlands: E. J. Brill, 1892–94), Vols. I and II. Here nearly every detail of late nineteenth-century practice is shown to conform to the scriptural injunctions.

6. *Li Ki* [*Chi*], James Legge trans. (Oxford, England: Oxford University Press, 1885), Book One, I, 1, pp. 62 ff.

7. *Ibid.,* Book Twenty-three, 5–7, pp. 257 f.

8. *Ibid.,* Book One, II, 3, p. 116.

9. *Ibid.,* Book One, I, 3, p. 82

10. *Ibid.* Book One, I, 2, pp. 71 f.

11. *Analects* II, 5.3.

12. *Mencius* IVA, 19.1, 2.

13. *Hsiao Ching* I.

14. *Ibid.,* X.

15. *Ibid.,* XI.

16. Ch'ü, T'ung-tsu, *Law and Society in Traditional China* (The Hague: Mouton & Co., Publishers, 1961), pp. 25 f.

17. *Li Ki* [*Chi*], Legge, trans., *op. cit.,* Book Ten, pp. 450 f, 453, and 458.

18. *Mencius* IVA, 26.1

19. *Li Ki* [*Chi*], Legge, trans., *op. cit.,* Book Ten I.20, pp. 458 f.

20. *Analects* I, 24.1.

21. *The Book of Documents,* Karlgren, trans., *op. cit.,* p. 26.

22. *Ibid.,* p. 35. Material in brackets supplied.

23. *Ibid.,* p. 21.

24. *Ibid.,* p. 24.

25. *Shih Ching,* Arthur Waley, trans., in *The Book of Songs* (London: Allen & Unwin, Ltd., 1937), p. 217. Material in brackets supplied.

26. *Analects* III, 12.1

27. *Ibid.,* VII, 20.

28. *Ibid.,* XI, 11.

29. *The Works of Hsuntze,* Homer Dubs, trans. (London: Arthur Probsthain, Publisher, 1928), pp. 244 f.

30. The most exhaustive treatment of the funeral rites will be found in de Groot, *op. cit.,* Vol. I, which devotes 237 pages to the subject. See, for an outline of the rites, the author's article, "Funeral rites in Taiwan," in the companion volume of readings (L. G. Thompson, ed., *The Chinese Way in Religion,* Dickenson, 1973, pp. 160–169).

31. *The I Li,* J. Steele, trans. (London: Arthur Probsthain, Publisher, 1917), Vol. II, pp. 9–12.

32. *Analects* XVII, 21.

33. Chiang, Monlin, *Tides From the West* (Taipei, Taiwan: China Culture Publishing Foundation, 1957), p. 9.

34. Chiang, Yee, *A Chinese Childhood* (New York: W. W. Norton & Company, Inc., 1963), pp. 9 ff.

Chapter 4

1. H. Maspero, "The Mythology of Modern China," in J. Hackin *et al., Asiatic Mythology* (New York: Thomas Y. Crowell Company, n.d.), p. 263.

2. *Ibid.,* p. 262.

3. The material in this section is largely based on my article "Notes on Religious Trends in Taiwan," *Monumenta Serica,* Vol. XXIII, 1964.

4. C. H. Plopper, *Chinese Religion Seen Through the Proverb* (Shanghai: The China Press, 1926), p. 33.

5. Maspero, *op. cit.,* p. 340.

6. David C. Graham, *Folk Religion in Southwest China* (Washington, D.C.: The Smithsonian Institution, 1961), p. 154, citing his own earlier article in the *Chinese Recorder,* July 1935, pp. 425 ff.

Chapter 5

1. The arrival of Confucian doctrines at this dominant position was a gradual process during two centuries B.C. See "The Victory of Han Confucianism," in *The History of the Former Han Dynasty by Pan Ku,* Homer H. Dubs, trans. and ed. (American Council of Learned Societies, 1944), Vol. II, pp. 341–352.

2. Tung, *An Interpretation of the Ancient Chinese Civilization, op. cit.,* pp. 18 f.

3. E. T. Williams, "The State Religion of China During the Manchu Dynasty," *Journal of the North China Branch, Royal Asiatic Society,* Vol. XLIV, 1913, p. 14.

4. Quotations from Yü-ch'üan Wang, "An Outline of the Central Government of the Former Han Dynasty," *Harvard Journal of Asiatic Studies,* Vol. 12, 1949, p. 151.

5. Hsieh, Pao-chao, *The Government of China (1644–1911)* (Baltimore, Md.: The Johns Hopkins Press, 1925), p. 142. Material in brackets supplied.

6. Williams, *op. cit.,* pp. 17 f.

7. *Analects* II, 3.

8. Shryock, *State Cult of Confucius,* pp. 176 f. Material in brackets supplied.

9. *Taiwan-hsien Chih,* 1720 ed.

10. *Ibid.*

11. *Ibid.*

12. *Ibid.*

Chapter 6

1. W. T. Chan, *A Source Book in Chinese Philosophy* (Princeton, N.J.: Princeton University Press, 1963), p. 373.

2. *Taiwan-hsien Chih, op. cit.*

3. Kenneth Ch'en *Buddhism in China: A Historical Survey* (Princeton, N.J.: Princeton University Press, 1964), pp. 310 F. Material in brackets supplied.

4. Junjiro Takakusu, *Essentials of Buddhist Philosophy* (2nd ed.) (Honolulu: University of Hawaii Press, 1949), pp. 135 f.

5. Ch'en, *op. cit.,* pp. 319 f.

6. Richard Robinson, trans., *Chinese Buddhist Verse* (London: John Murray (Publishers), Ltd., 1954), p. 43.

7. Takakusu, *op. cit.,* p. 163.

8. W. T. Chan, trans., *The Way of Lao Tzu* (Indianapolis, Ind.: The Bobbs-Merrill Company, Inc., 1963), p. 159.

9. *Ibid.,* p. 188.

10. *Ibid.,* p. 16.

11. *Ibid.,* p. 199.

12. *Chuang Tzu: Basic Writings,* Burton Watson, trans. (New York: Columbia University Press, 1964), p. 26.

13. *Ibid.,* p. 27.

14. *Ibid.,* p. 119. Material in Brackets supplied.

15. *Chuang Tzu,* Fung, Yu-lan, trans. (Shanghai: Commercial Press, 1933), p. 112. Material in brackets supplied.

16. Homer H. Dubs, trans., "The Beginnings of Alchemy," *Isis,* Vol. 38, 1947, pp. 67 ff. Material in brackets by the translator.

17. L.C. Wu and T. L. Davis, trans., "An Ancient Chinese Treatise on Alchemy Entitled Ts'an T'ung Ch'i," *Isis,* Vol. 18, 1932, p. 255. Material in brackets and parentheses by the translators.

18. *Ibid.,* pp. 260 f. Material in brackets and parentheses by the translators.

19. "Pao P'u Tzu," E. Feifel, trans., *Monumenta Serica,* Vol. VI, 1941, pp. 158 ff.

20. *Ibid.,* pp. 209 ff. Material in parentheses supplied.

21. *Ibid.,* p. 9 f.

22. Arthur Waley, "Notes on Chinese Alchemy," *Bulletin of the School of Oriental and African Studies* (University of London), Vol. 6, Pt. 1, 1930, pp. 15 f. Material in brackets supplied.

23. *Chuang Tzu,* Fung, trans., *op. cit.,* p. 56. Material in brackets supplied.

24. *Mencius* VIIA, 4.1. Material in brackets supplied.

25. *Chuang Tzu,* Fung, trans., *op. cit.,* p. 43.

26. *Ibid.,* p. 54 f.

27. *Ibid.,* p. 119 f.

28. The sixty-third generation Chang T'ien Shih fled from the Communists, who confiscated his ancestral estates on Lung-hu Shan (mountain) in Kiangsi province, going first to Hong Kong, and eventually to Taiwan, where he died (around 1970?). Burkhardt, *Chinese Creeds and Customs, op. cit.,* pp. 132 ff, has an article on him, illustrated with a portrait. See also Holmes Welch's article, "The Chang T'ien Shih and Taoism in China," *Journal of Oriental Studies* (University of Hong Kong), Vol. 4, 1957–58, pp. 188–212, which includes the author's report of his personal visit to the Taoist leader in Taiwan. A distant relative has succeeded him as sixty-fourth generation "heavenly master."

INDEX

[Approximate pronunciations of Chinese words are in square brackets.]